Learners Rule!

Giving them a voice improves the culture of their classroom

By Bill Zima

ZEA PUBLISHING

Table of Contents

Introduction

The fall of 2007 started like any other school year. Students and teachers entered the building tanned, light in spirit, all while carrying a sense of anticipation for what the year had in store. The only difference was that the administration decided to focus on the number of students who were failing math. I was part of that administrative team.

Over the summer, I reviewed the previous three year's math grades. We had nearly a third of our students failing 7th grade math. This was unacceptable, to say the least. When I asked the math team at our opening meetings why this was happening, the response was clear; the students did not know their basic facts. They were coming to us underprepared to handle the requirements of middle school math. After blaming this program or that one, we were not even sure which program was being used in the 7 elementary schools that fed our middle school, we decided we needed to do something about it. So we researched, found, and purchased skill remediation software. We were going to fix it.

At the first quarter marking period, we actually had a slight increase in the number of students failing. We were using the programs correctly and at a time in the schedule that did not affect their class instruction. Why were we still seeing increases in the number of failing students?

When the math team was asked this question again, the answer became that the students were not doing their homework. If only they did it we would not have this issue. I asked if it was the work completion or loss of skills from not having appropriate practice that was making the difference. They felt it was both. "I have students who do well on the tests but won't do a bit of homework. We can't pass those students without doing any work. Where would they learn responsibility?"

So, we created The Homework Cafe. Students lost socialization time during lunch and instead had to eat their food while completing their homework in a different room. We had a staff member monitor the cafe. We did not need a teacher as the work was expected to be done independently. If our Cafe Monitor noticed that students struggled with understanding, she sent a note to the teacher informing him or her of the need for extra support with the content.

As we reached the end of the second quarter, hopes were high that more students would pass their math class. When grades were calculated and posted, we once again experienced a slight uptick in the number of failures. Needless to say we were all very disappointed.

At the next math department meeting, I announced that if anyone knew why students are failing, please let me know so I can get some donuts and coffee and we can find a solution. As one of the teachers left the meeting he paused to say, "I like Boston Cream donuts."

"What?" I asked with a surprised tone. I was not expecting such a quick response to my offer.

"I know why we have issues," he said in a casual tone. "I will tell you tomorrow morning."

So the next morning, in the dark of a cold January morning in Maine, we met in my office. The little conference table was snug into one of the corners in an attempt to maximize the room to move. This arrangement made it possible for only two chairs to be placed at the table. We each took a chair, I handed him a Boston Cream donut and coffee and got right to the point. I was not interested in small talk since I had not been able to stop thinking about what he could have possibly figured out so quickly. "So, what's up?"

"Well. It's actually quite simple," he said in a tone that made it hard to tell if he was serious or sarcastic. If it was so simple, how have we not seen it before. He continued, "We do not know why students are failing."

"WHAT," I heard myself respond in a tone just below a shout. Was he kidding. I lost sleep last night pondering what he was going to say and this is what I get. I stopped for donuts and coffee and got excited just to hear we don't know why students are failing. He is now on my short list of people I tune out when they share their thoughts. Collecting my nerves so I did not seem out of control I said, "Thanks. I appreciate your perspective. Enjoy the donut."

As I got up to leave he chuckled and said, "You are not hearing what I am saying." He paused for dramatic effect. "We do not know why students are failing." He said it slower and more deliberate. This time, his words leapt right into my ears and kickstarted my brain. Slowly my face shifted from disappointment to a smile of understanding. He was right. We had no idea.

"Yes," I finally said. "We are teaching textbooks, chapters, and courses. We are not teaching kids. We wait for the struggle, encourage them to try harder, but continue moving through the book. We never stop to patch the hole. We never give it another thought."

He had hit a nerve. As educators we never spent time talking about what we actually hoped kids learned from the textbook. When kids struggled, we hoped they would have more success on the next chapter or unit so their average grade would increase. As I reflect on my career, I can see myself telling parents, "Well its okay. He hated physics but we just started ecology and I think his work on this unit will bring his overall grade up." What was our focus? The grade or the bit of knowledge making the grade? I finally saw the answer.

The problem with the current plan of addressing curriculum was we had no idea how deep the hole in their learning went. Was it a superficial wound that would scab over and eventually be undetectable? Or was it deep and festering? An injury to learning that is so deep it never quite heals correctly only to come back later in life as as either a deep infection causing future learning to be slowed or an unknown pain whose origins are a mystery.

Thanks to the effective strategies supported in the research of Response to Intervention (RTI), we were able to find some of the "infections" in their learning early, and with intense support, could cure them. It was the missed learning due to unknown issues that arose a few years down the learning path that caused the most headaches. Something needed to be done.

We ended the year creating a plan to help us begin to shift our system away from textbook chapters and unit tests to one that had the students meet standards. We were hoping to create a system that communicates to students, parents, and the student's future teachers exactly what the student knows and can do while also identifying what learning still presents challenges. Instead of moving an entire group forward and creating a single learning opportunity regardless of what the individual student entered the grade-level with, there was hope that we could differentiate instruction and truly give the student what he or she needs. We now knew that without clear targets of learning, we had no idea what we were aiming for.

We spent the 2008-2009 school year unpacking the Maine Learning Results to get at what students should know and be able to do in all content areas. Teachers were given time to meet as grade level, content area specialists and define their learning targets. Other researchers have called them Enduring Understandings. We simply said "what are the things you want students to know when you bump into them on the street in 10 years." If you won't care then, don't care now. In April, we had the document ready to go. The Framework of Skills articulated to us, our parents and of course our students, what we wanted students to know and be able to do in each year and in each content area while they were in our middle school.

In early May, a group of teachers approached the administration and asked if they could pilot being fully standards-based during the next school year. They were a group of elite runners, not afraid to be out in front of the crowd. They embraced ambiguity and loved creating a path. We happily supported their request.

In late May, I met with Rick Schreiber from ReInventing Schools Coalition (RISC). The State of Maine was looking for districts to pilot moving to a personal-mastery system. Rick explained what RISC had done in Alaska, Colorado and California and what was the hope for Maine. That began a very important relationship for our school.

As the 2009-2010 school year began, the pilot team faced early challenges as managing a classroom of independent learners was not the same as the traditional classroom. The core of personal mastery was that students worked at their readiness level and moved forward only when they had demonstrated mastery of a particular learning goal. Trying to manage this innovative approach to learning while maintaining a traditional classroom was awkward. Something needed to change. But what?

In November of 2009, two of the teachers from the pilot team went to a Classroom Design and Delivery (CDD) training with RISC. When they returned to their classrooms, they began implementing some of the strategies they learned. The class was magically transformed. Once the teachers stopped managing a traditional classroom and instead began overseeing the culture, students began to take off.

We stumbled across one of the important lessons of implementing any reform in education whether it is a full scale system shift like moving to personal mastery learning or adding writer's workshop to your english classes, culture is the lynchpin.

This book attempts to explain in story form what a class might experience as they work to build a culture of learners. Alex, the newly hired math teacher, works to establish a strong culture while his mentor, Josh, who is struggling with his own desire to improve his classroom, watches. After initially struggling to understand, Josh takes the lead in helping Alex to see that his plan for building culture is something more then simple luck.

Even though the book is heavily influenced by research in education, business, and neuroscience and also what I have experienced and seen as a teacher, administrator, and consultant, all characters appearing in this work are fictitious. Any resemblance to real persons, living or dead, is purely coincidental.

This book is meant to be a work of Tactical Fiction, it provides a plan for promoting a desired end result by using a narrative structure. I hope you enjoy the book and the tale of Alex and Josh. I will be writing others to help create a narrative of what a classroom or school would look or sound like when implementing all four of the lenses of customized learning; curriculum, instruction, assessment, and of course cultureIf you have comments or questions that you would like to share, please contact me zimaw@yahoo.com.

Thanks.

Bill Zima
Twitter: @zimaw

learnersrule.com

Check out the webpage for videos and text to further support
how to build and keep alive a strong culture for learners.

1

Coaches Meeting

"Hey Beaner! How was your summer?" trumpeted Kevin Hill as his 6 foot 4inch, 250 pound frame filled the door to the classroom.

"Great. How was yours?" Responded Joshua Bean in a calm voice. He was not surprised by Kevin's entrance as he had grown used to it over the many years the two have been teaching together.

"Not too bad. I had to take a few classes for recertification but otherwise it was filled with football camps and conditioning. You know, the stuff I really love outside of teaching." Kevin is a social studies teacher and the middle school's head football coach. Even though he has been doing it for the last 10 years, he still feels the need to let his colleagues know how dedicated he is to the student athletes.

"I was not able to take any classes over the summer. I am hoping that I can attend a few workshops this fall," Josh said with a sense of disappointment in his voice.

"You," said Kevin in a tone you might hear in a movie when the hero notices that his arch enemy is actually his best friend. "You don't need to take any classes. Heck, you are the best math teacher in our district. I might even say in our State. You have been teaching for what, 22, 23 years?"

"This is the beginning of my 30th year," Josh helped his friend remember. He had started only a year after the coach, but Kevin always liked to think of himself as the elder statesman of the school.

"Wow. Really? In that time you have been teacher of the year twice for the district and once a runner-up for the State. Around 35 percent of your students go on to take AP classes in high school. You are a favorite of students, parents and colleagues. You have been asked by the Department of Education several times to help work on the standards for math. I believe you could write the math textbook you are teaching. What could someone possibly teach you?" Kevin said rhetorically while patting him on the back as though he were one of his athletes.

"I just feel I am missing something. I feel like there is more out there for me to understand. You know, so I can help my students prepare for the futures that lie in front of them."

"Oh no. Not this conversation again," said a voice in a much less troop rallying cry then Kevin's. Both men whirled to see that Angela Clout had come into the classroom.

"Hey Angela. How's that son of yours?" asked Kevin as if her boy was the most important child in the community.

"He is good Kevin. Thanks for asking."

"Quite a football player. Has he signed a pro contract yet?" Kevin asked.

"No," Angela said with a sense of sarcasm. "The last I knew the NFL still has a clause that students need to attend college for a few years before joining a professional team. Seeing as he is just starting his eighth grade year, we have not had many recruiters knocking at our door."

"Oh but they will. Maybe not tomorrow but they will come'" Kevin said while giving her a wink.

"Maybe not tomorrow? Definitely not tomorrow. I am not ready to even think about that. Let us get through adolescence first," Angela said with a sense of dread.

"Well, once he joins my team, we will dominate the conference," Kevin roared while looking up to the ceiling with a clenched fist.

Now Josh joined in, "Didn't we redo our middle school program 15 years ago to make it less about winning and more about athlete development?"

"Always the dream killer," Kevin said while slowly turning his gaze to the floor. "But, since you are the boss, I will do what you say."

"You were instrumental in the change in programming. 'Fighting for what you believed was right' is what you said to the school board," stated Josh

"Just because I think it is better for kids in the long run does not mean I miss the days of domination through sports," explained Kevin.

"So what was this that I heard as I entered the room," Angela said hoping to move the conversation away from sports. She gets enough of it all year during their teaching team's lunch. "Were you going on again about how you feel something is missing from your teaching. Didn't we talk about this at your wife's birthday bar-b-cue? I had thought by your third serving of ribs and your Frye's Leap IPA, you had resolved that you are a fantastic teacher and that you should just focus on doing more of what you already do and give yourself a break."

"Yeah. I know I said that. But I was just trying to release the conversation so it stopped being about me," Josh said sheepishly. "I woke up the next morning still feeling as though there is more I can do. I am not looking to redo the entire class or completely overhaul my teaching. I just think there is something I can do to better help prepare the kids for the world they will face. It is quite different from when we graduated college," he said emphatically. Then looking at both of his colleagues he quickly added, "well me and this old sports star. You, Angela are a bit closer in age to our recent grads."

"How nice of you to say," Angela said giving her hair a model's flick. "But in reality I graduated college 15 years ago and high school almost 20 years ago. Many of the technologies the students now use never existed. The way the world communicates is vastly different. I look at what my husband has to deal with in his work place. If he does not keep up with the latest in social media, he does not expand the audience for the minor league baseball team. And that bums out his bosses. They love expanding their product," Angela shared with a slight hint of sarcasm. She was a fan of the team but was always amazed at how much money was spent trying to attract and keep fans. Sometimes she wished public schools could spend that kind of money promoting all the great things they do. She continued,

"Marketing is so different today compared to when he started. Now, having interns every summer certainly helps him stay current with the technology trends. But our students will continue to face a horizontal world. No that's not it. Face a," she paused and glanced to the ceiling as though the phrase she wanted was painted on the ceiling tiles, "Flat World."

"Wait a minute," interrupted Kevin. "You had a bar-b-cue for Gloria's birthday, and you did not invite me"

"Of course we did," stated Josh."Both you and Jane were invited. You were heading to the football hall of fame that weekend. It was your once every four year trip to the Mecca of Sports, as you like to say."

"Oh yeah. Did I tell you about the new display. It was about Superbowl"…

"Anyway. Angela you are absolutely right." Josh needed to cut Kevin off. He has shared the story with everyone. After the third time politely sitting through it and the next two times letting him know he had already heard it, Josh now simply carries on with what he needs to say. Kevin eventually stops. "Kids today have such a different reality. How do you manage it with your son?"

"It is hell," Angela shared in her best demon voice. "When he is not talking or texting on his phone he is Face-timing, Skyping or posting on some new social site. Seems those things pop up almost daily. No matter how hard I try to control it, he finds a way to connect. I do not want to discourage it as he is learning how to communicate in the world he will live in. But I also want some other control. I know when I was his age, I wanted to be connected to my friends 24/7. The only thing was that no means of doing that was possible. I wish I had a crystal ball so I could see the future impacts of all this."

"Hey gents and lady. How is it going this fine morning?" said Dale Kellogg, the school's principal as he busted into the room.

"Gee Dale. You got a tie on already?" said Kevin with a sense of disappointment usually reserved for those people most likely to let you down.

"Well, I want to look the part as parents come in to register their students. School is open in a week. We have been busy."

Kevin decided to add a little sting, "Have you ever considered relaxing and doing a little business casual during the summers?"

"Well, I have already had the Administrative retreat and we have our Leadership Team meeting tomorrow. You're coming right?" Dale inquired of Josh who simply nodded. "Besides, I enjoy putting on a tie. It is sort of like putting on a uniform and your game face as you meet the crosstown rival on the old grid iron."

"No. Not really. Not at all the same. And we do not go to the malt shop with Archie and Jughead after the big game either. Crosstown rivals on the grid iron," Kevin said in a deep mocking voice.

"Well everyone gets ready for their challenges in their own way," Dale retorted. "We all have different big games," he finished by making air quotation marks around the last two words.

"Tell him Angela. Football is the only big game in town." Kevin knew he was stretching but was looking for some back up. Even though Dale and Kevin had a good relationship and a strong, mutual respect, they had grown up together and still felt that one-upping each other, as they once did on the playground, was a necessary activity.

"I believe you know my stance on this. You and my husband are obsessed with football, but I believe it is not for all kids. Quite frankly, I enjoy watching my daughter's soccer games more then football games. They move so much faster."

"Traitor," Kevin mumbled under his breath.

Dale decided to get to the point of his visit. "Josh, have you made contact with Alex Winter yet?"

"I have. We are meeting later today in his room. Anything specific you want me to talk with him about?"

"No," Dale said in a tone that seemed as though he was still thinking about it. "Simply make him as great as you are and we are all set. He comes highly recommended. His references were stellar, as you know Josh since you were on the interview committee. I think he will be a great addition to our math team. Simply help him get oriented. Talk with him about our curriculum and assessment philosophy and show him how to take attendance. Just once before I retire I want to get the school-wide, daily attendance done correctly. I am sure you will be fine Josh. I will catch you guys later. Hope the team is ready for some football," Dale sang the Monday Night Football theme while exiting the room and patting Kevin on the shoulder.

"Everyone has their game day," Kevin said in a teasing tone when he was sure Dale was out of ear shot. "Is he for real? How can he possibly confuse the preparation for an athletic competition, the display of the human form in all its glory, pushing for the extra oomph, with the simple task of getting ready to be a school administrator."

After hesitating slightly, Josh decided to chime in with his opinion, "Dale is a great principal." Josh was not the type to offer his opinions. He really did not like controversy. He usually agreed with everyone even if it was not true. Last year he agreed to liking Law and Order, Special Victims' Unit even though he had never seen it. But to avoid having to defend his opinion, he simply went along. He figures that is why he became a math teacher. You get to defend with proofs and theorems and not opinions.

"You did not have to deal with him in high school!" Kevin said with a sense of despair.

"No," Josh said, "But remember some of the principals we have had over the years? All the top down dictators. The ones who thought they had all the answers and it was this program or that program. I love that Dale knows nothing works for all kids. There are no magic potions in education. He gives teachers the flexibility to use the art and science of teaching. I feel more free to explore and find strategies to work with kids. Just as long as they pass through our agreed upon philosophies." Josh walked towards the door and shut it so they would not get any more interruptions. "I have truly enjoyed the last few years. Ever since Dale came here. I think that is what is pushing me to think there is even more. He has given me the latitude to be innovative and when something does not work, he is there to consult with."

"Wow. No wonder you are on the leadership team," Kevin joked.

"I think it is more than that," Angela chimed in to give support to Dale but even more for Josh. "He truly respects us and understands what it is like to be a professional who has a personal life. He really models our code of respect."

"I know," Kevin conceded. "I would never want to go back to the pre-Dale years. And you talk about someone who knows my deepest secrets and what I was like in my early years and still continues to give me responsibility. I am a fan of his as well. But if anyone ever repeats that," he paused as he noticed the clock. "Dang. I gotta go. Have equipment hand-out in an hour at the high school. Need to get ready for the year. I will catch you guys later if you are still here. Are you still planning to host the Labor Day Bar-b-cue?" he asked while glancing over his shoulder, back to his colleagues.

Josh nodded.

"Good. Josh, are you inviting the new guy and his family. Love to meet him." With that he was gone as abruptly as he entered.

"So who is the new guy?" Angela inquired.

"He is younger, maybe around 32. Has a small family he moved over the summer. He was not always a teacher but since joining the ranks has made quite a splash. He made one heck of an impression at the interviews and he will also be coaching our boy's soccer team. He should be a good addition to our school."

"That's great to hear." Angela said with a definite sense of relief. "We do not get much turnover here and when Grant announced his retirement last year, I was worried about how it would impact our culture. You know, we are a tight group."

"Dale was very aware of that and asked the interview committee to make sure it was someone who could live up to the school's code of conduct: Focused, Respectful and Responsible. I think Alex will be great."

"We are a good school with a great reputation," Angela shared, "and a high school who sends many of its students to good colleges. I hope he can continue the great work Grant and you started. Although it would be great if he can match your number of AP students."

"Yeah. That is a good percentage of students. But what about all the other kids. Am I helping them?"

"Is this going to be the theme for this year?" Angela was now becoming annoyed and her voice was not hiding it. "Your job is to get students ready to be successful in high school and then college. If students choose not to engage in what you have to teach them, then why is that your fault? They need to take responsibility for themselves. It's your job to give them opportunities and it is up to them to be responsible and do it. And the opportunities you give and your instruction is top notch. Now I need to go and get some things done in my room. I do not want this all year, or worse, the next few years before you retire. You have nothing left to prove. You are already better than the majority of teachers. So don't put pressure on yourself"

Not wanting to be disagreeable, Josh simply nodded. He knew that he had to get going since it was almost time to meet with his new mentee, Alex Winter. But a feeling was still gnawing at him. A feeling that there must be more he can do to help prepare the students of today. He knew he did a wonderful job for the college bound. But what about all the others. Could he simply say it is their issue for not wanting to go to college? Could he let a 12 year old have so much control over his life or should he get in there and help them see the value of learning? That led him to wonder if he was in fact creating college students and not learners.

Much like the hero in a movie needs to discover for himself the hidden path that leads to his greatness, the path Josh was seeking had not become realized. Little did he know that the meeting he was about to have was actually the first step on his journey.

2

The Newly Acquired

It was noon and Josh needed to head down the hall to meet his new colleague, Alex Winter. He has not seen him since the interview and only spoke with his wife briefly to welcome them to the community and establish this meeting time. Josh truly enjoyed listening to Alex promote himself at the interview. He felt that Alex has a knack for how to make mathematics sensible to students. He was also intrigued about something he had said in the interview, that math should be applied and not simply assessed. Josh liked how that sounded but wanted to know more about what it meant. That is why he volunteered so quickly when Dale asked for volunteers to be Alex's mentor. He knew he could learn from him.

As Josh entered Alex's new room, he was surprised to see him sitting at a table in the middle of the room. The walls of the room were bare except for the mandatory evacuation poster, the school schedule, his diplomas and a poster of Ryne Sandberg, the Hall of Fame second baseman for the Chicago Cubs. The room did not look or feel empty however. Plants of different varieties must have helped. The walls looked more like the scoreboard at the ballpark as the players arrive. It will come to life, happily communicating the activities of the game to the fans, but currently it was blank.

The table Alex was sitting at was higher then the students' desks and had 5 stools evenly placed around it. The one Alex was using had a back, the others did not. It was something he had never seen in a classroom. It looked more like seating you find at a TGI Fridays. If Alex was eating hot wings and cheering on the Red Sox, Josh would have been convinced he had been transported out of the building.

Learners Rule

The Students' desks were clustered in groups. Some four, some five, and even some in groups of six. In the front and center of the classroom, where Josh kept his LCD projector, overhead, and document camera there were no seats. Just a big open area covered with a rather interesting rug that reminded Josh of something he once had in his family room. The browns and oranges matched well with the wood paneling decor of a seventies home. Josh could not help but begin to wonder where in fact Alex lectured from. The students did not seem to be able to have eye contact with him. Who will sit at the big table? If kids are sitting there, no one in the back group will be able to see the board from their desks. Josh convinced himself that Alex was not quite settled and would arrange the desks at a later time to more closely resemble a math classroom. Alex chose instead to sit down and take a break. Maybe he was working on his seating chart and would label the desks before putting them into rows.

Alex turned quickly as he got the sense that someone was behind him. Josh quickly turned his gaze from the front to meet with Alex's eyes. He smiled quickly in an attempt to hide any sign that he was concerned with the condition of the room. "Hey Alex. How are you?" Josh said in an excited tone while extending his hand.

Alex popped from his stool. It was tall enough to just support the full extent of his six foot frame so he did not have to jump down. Simply slide off. "I am great Josh. How are you. Haven't seen you since the interviews in May. I really enjoyed that opportunity." The two shook hands.

"Me too," Josh commented. "How was the move? Cannot be easy with a little one and a pregnant wife?"

"No. Not at all. My wife and daughter flew up. My father in-law and I had the pleasure of packing the old house into the U-Haul and driving it up here."

"Twelve hundred mile drive with your father in-law in the cab of a truck? Man, that had to be tough."

"Well. It wasn't so bad. He is a very interested and intelligent guy so conversation can flow easily. Don't get me wrong, I did consider taking our family car off of the trailer and driving that to find some refuge. But all in all it was good. Just excited to be here."

"Where did you find a place to settle?"

"We bought a house right here in the community," Alex said with sincere enthusiasm. "This is a perfect sized city for us. I cannot do rural as I like to be able to walk to get a cup of coffee in the morning and the minor league baseball team is right here. I love baseball."

"Me too. But I thought you wanted to be our soccer coach?" Josh said nervously wondering if he got that wrong in the interview. The school had lost soccer coaches every year for the last five. Hard to build a good program for kids if there is no consistency. He had hoped that Alex was to be the solution.

"Oh yes. If that is still available?" Alex was now becoming nervous that he had misinterpreted the conversation during the interview.

"It's yours if you want it."

"Good," Alex said as he exhaled heavily to send the stress that quickly grew in his body out into the lithosphere. "I played soccer in high school and think it is a wonderful sport for kids. Baseball is my favorite of the TV sports."

"One of our friends is the marketing director for the minor league team. We like to make group outings to the games. I will let you know and you can join us. It is fun. They are affiliated with the Red Sox. I assume the Cubs are your team?" Josh asked while pointing at the poster of Ryne Sandberg.

"Yeah. The Cubs have taught me a lot about winning and losing, more about losing, and how to keep everything in perspective. Even though I have not followed the team very closely since I left Chicago ten years ago, I am still hopeful that one day we see a World Series Champion Cubs team. Sandberg to me represents a great player with great character. No matter how difficult things may seem, doing your personal best pays long term benefits. His team never made it to the World Series, but he always tried his hardest, won the MVP in 1984, and was elected to the Hall of Fame."

"Not bad at all." Josh could see that Alex was enjoying the trip down memory lane and had an insight into what motivation meant to him. He knew Alex believed in effort and not fixed ability. He could have talked baseball and philosophy all day but he needed to get to work. "Dale has assigned me as your mentor. That pretty much means I am your go to guy for any questions you might have about our school, our procedures, paperwork, certification. You know. Just about anything you need to know. I am here for you.

Alex smiled and said, "Thats great. Thanks Josh. Every school has its own system for the lunch count, attendance, paperwork and all of the unwritten practices and of course politics."

"Well the good news," Josh began while adjusting his position on the stool to attempt to redistribute the pressure on his backside, "is that this group of teachers is an absolutely tremendous group of people. While we occasionally have frustration amongst staff, it never turns into gossip or politicking. Everyone is so supportive of each other. I think that is why the school is so successful."

Alex was relieved to hear that. In his previous school, the teacher's room was often filled with negativity and back biting. Even when the principal entered the room it continued. He would make comments about how a particular teacher handled a discipline issue with a student. Pointing out some else's mistakes as a sign of idiocy usually got the group to roar. Not very strong leadership. Little did they know that when they were not present, they were the target of his comments. The room grew so negative and toxic that Alex began to eat in his room instead of the teacher's room. At first it was lonely, but then others began to join him. Soon it was the place to be for lunch. The positive energy was shared in stories of family and games of cribbage. The Toxic Trio as Alex liked to think of the rulers of the lunchroom culture, probably wondered where everyone had gone.

"That's good," Alex said with a sense of relief. "My old school had grown toxic until changes were made. The saddest part was that it boiled down to the actions of three people out of a staff of 120. And the principal was blinded by how his actions affected the environment."

"Dale is very aware of the culture in the building," Josh reassured. "He talks about it frequently in our leadership meetings. He is not perfect. No person is. But if you notice something you can point it out to him and he will consider adjusting. It helps that the teachers and staff really want a good working environment. One full of support, so they are willing to try new things in the name of continuous improvement. I have not worked at many other places, but have heard stories from my friends."

"Wonderful," said Alex with a big smile on his face.

There was a slight lull in the conversation so Josh turned it back to how Alex was settling in. "So, what are you working on?"

"Oh, I am working on the random sorting of students into the classroom," Alex said with enthusiasm typically reserved for someone who was about to show pictures of his children. "I always like to start with a lesson at the very beginning. You see, I take these old calendar pictures, cut them into 4,5 or 6 pieces and then as the students enter the room, I greet them and hand them each a piece. I don't tell them what they are for. But taped in the group of desks is the same picture but uncut. Many of the students ask me what they are suppose to do but I simply smile and welcome them to class again. Sometimes I simply shrug."

"Wow," interrupted Josh. "Some of my students would not like that. They want to know they are doing it right, what ever right is. Do you get worried that you are stressing the students right off the bat?".

"I have those students too," Alex said. "But I am attempting to get them to think without every step being spelled out. Sometimes teachers over script learning opportunities. We forget to look for easy ways for students to think and instead overwrite the process so they can't make a mistake. I believe the process of thinking is as important as the product. Let the students struggle!" Alex said while raising his right hand into the air as though he was a king making a real decree. "The students need to make an inference that the piece I gave them is actually guiding them to their seat. It might be simple and slightly silly, but I like to start the year by showing them that they can figure it out." Alex knew he had not seen anyone ever get over stressed. Usually, once they figure it out, even if they got the idea on what to do from someone else, they feel a sense of accomplishment. He continued explaining, "Before the full group conversation begins, I walk the room and give students who might be in the wrong seat a bit of encouragement and a hint."

"Then what," asked Josh who found himself leaning forward like a fan hoping the break away results in a goal.

"Once all the students are in, we talk about what they did to figure it out. It begins our first conversation about problem solving and about using the strategy of trial and error. I have them write their names on a diagram of the classroom and those become their seats. More thinking involved than simply being told where to go. And it really is a fun way to randomly mix the students. Then we begin to establish the class ground rules."

"Sounds great. I like posting the ground rules in front of the class so it is visible when I am in my lecture spot. Do you have your rules ready?" Josh thought he found a way to ask about the room layout without coming out and suggesting he had concerns about how his new mentor will teach.

"Nope. Not yet. I need to get input from the students first," Alex said without even hesitating.

The ease with which Alex made this comment caused Josh to be both concerned and interested. To express with so much confidence, he must have tried this arrangement before. If he did, he must have had success with it. Josh's experience had always been that once the students got comfortable in his class, the rules they helped to create dissolved. Besides, kids knew what was expected of them in school. Most kids did the right thing every day. The others just needed a swift consequence to get them back on track. Even though Josh had reservations about the plan, he did not want to crush Alex's confidence so decided not to comment. Josh would later come to remember this initial conversation and realize how close he came to making a mistake by commenting on Alex's discipline plan.

"Well I got to go," Josh said. "I have to double check my equipment for fall sports so I can start as soon as I want." He shifted his weight from his rear to his feet and found himself standing. "That was better then getting up out of my desk chair. It was so easy." He glanced back down at the chair.

"Great," Alex said. "I really appreciate you taking the time to come down and offer support so my transition is easier. I am sure once the students are here next week, the questions will fly."

They shook hands and Josh moved to the door. "Oh by the way," he said turning back around to face Alex. "We are having a BBQ at my house on Monday afternoon. You know, a little Labor Day thing. We would love it if you and Meg would join us. Many of our colleagues will be there and it would be a great chance to get to know them before the first day of school."

"I can check with Meg, but I think since we know very few people in town, we do not have plans."

"Great. Two o'clock. Bring your swimsuits and something to drink. We love micro-brews so feel free to have a beer or two with us. I will provide the meat and condiments. It is the last official day of Bratwurst season, so that is what we will have."

"Awesome. I love Brats but had no idea there was a season," Alex said with confusion.

"Not always the most widely known of seasons. Had a friend who started me on celebrating it years back and now I keep it up. It begins the Friday of Memorial Day weekend and ends with Labor Day Monday."

"We shall see you then. Thanks again," Alex said with a smile on his face. He began believing that his decision to move could turn out to be a good one.

Josh turned to look at the room one last time. He had been such a strong supporter of Alex since the hiring was done. He boasted often that he would stake his reputation on what a great addition Alex was going to be. But now he began to wonder if Alex fell victim to the education fads syndrome. Jumping on all the bandwagons that move away from the tried and true approaches of a traditional classroom. Even though Josh himself was beginning to believe he could do more for all of his students than the stand and deliver model would allow, he worried Alex's youth would make him vulnerable to ignoring the long trail of successful strategies. Hopefully he would not be prey for people trying to sell books and programs. Little did Josh know how much his leadership would be tested by the addition of Alex.

3

Preseason Doubt

Josh and his wife Gloria were busy in the kitchen prepping for the bar-b-cue. It was important to have all of the food ready to go so they could spend as much time outside with their friends as possible.

Their house was a simple, 3-bedroom ranch. Choosing never to become house poor, they decided money was better spent on friends and family.

Gloria could tell Josh was distracted by something. The Red Sox were already losing to the Yankees, 3-0 in the bottom of the first inning and not a word of frustration was spoken. Normally he would have been beside himself yelling about the 'over paid bums'. Today though, he was silent.

"Be careful not to cut those onions too thin. Remember last year we lost them all to the fire gods," Gloria suggested.

"Yeah. I remember. Will do," he said in a tone more reminiscent of Eeyore then of a person who loves to entertain.

"Red Sox are doing great," Gloria tested.

"Yeah, they are."

That was the piece of evidence she needed. "Alright. What is going on with you?" Gloria demanded.

Josh snapped his head towards her and spoke as if he woke from a dream, "What? Me? Nothing. Did you say something?"

"Yes," Gloria said walking towards him and wrapping her arms around his waist. "I mentioned how well the Sox were playing and you agreed. Do you know they are losing to the Yankees?"

"Just kind of in my own little world thinking about tomorrow," Josh said. "I have a sense of dread and am not sure why."

"You love the first day of school. It has been your favorite day since I met you," Gloria said finishing with a quick peck of support on his cheek and turning back to the salsa.

"I know," Josh said with a slight tinge of confusion. "Teaching is one of the few professions where you get a fresh beginning every year. You get a chance to improve upon what you did last year."

"And unlike sports," Gloria interrupted, "you don't age out."

"True. Unless you choose to be an educator who is more of a bench sitter. You know, always approaching things in the same way year after year. Choosing not to check your practice and adjust based on new evidence. Glad I am a teacher and not a baseball player. I cannot imagine how much stress it is to be in your mid-thirties and have people argue whether you are washed up." Josh was attempting to change the subject. Hoping to distract from the fact that he did not know what was really bothering him.

Gloria did not let it rest. She could tell from his conversation that his thoughts were scattered. "Well, if you are excited about the first day then what could it be?"

"I don't really know," Josh began. "It seems to center on my thoughts about Alex Winter."

"The new math teacher you are mentoring?" Gloria asked.

"Yes, him. When we interviewed him he seemed so on top of his game. Really presented himself as someone who knew how to make math comprehensible to kids. His references were spotless and all gave him enthusiastic support. He is very personable and will also be able to help the school with our athletic teams."

"So what exactly is the problem, Josh?" Gloria said in a tone so thick with sarcasm he actually considered not answering her.

"Well, I have told everyone how wonderful he is and now I fear he might not be able to live up to it. How will that look?"

"Are you more concerned about your reputation or of the success of Alex?" Gloria inquired causing Josh to place his knife down and take a deep breath.

"I don't know. I hope it is about helping him fit in. But that doesn't feel right. There is something else."

"What is it about him that caused you to turn. You were so supportive of him all summer. Telling me often about this 'Math Superman' you hired."

"See! it is things like that," Josh said with panic in his voice while frantically wiggling his pointed finger at Gloria. "Why did I say things like that. Did I raise everyone's expectations too high and he will falter?"

"Why are you now thinking he will falter?" Gloria probed him again.

"When I stopped by his room the other day, the walls were bare, the desks were not in rows and he was not creating a seating chart."

"Are those signs of dooooooom in the teaching world?" Gloria said, drawing out the word doom for dramatic effect.

"No." Josh said raising the ending in a sarcastic, upward slide so it sounded musical. "But I fear he is either non-traditional or unorganized or both. To start the year without everything in place, just puts one behind. And it is really difficult to catch up. Hasn't he learned that in his five years of teaching?"

"Well, I cannot speak to his being unorganized. Only time will show that. But why does he have to be traditional? What does that even mean?" Gloria said. She often did not understand teaching lingo. She wondered if they had a different understanding of the word 'traditional'. Gloria had not been in a classroom since she finished her MBA. After schooling and marrying Josh, she opened a bakery shop. The rest of her training was done on the job. She learned much more about accounting and marketing theories by applying them in her day to day operations of her bakery shop. With a bit of luck and her constant monitoring of industry trends, Gloria was well placed to take advantage of the coffee house explosion of the early nineties. Her business grew from a single store to four in the greater metropolitan area and even 3 more stores in a nearby city. That was as big as she wanted to expand. Josh and Gloria's oldest daughter, Erin, was finishing school and would happily return home to manage the business. First for a few years with mom and then on her own. A gradual release of control.

"Traditional means honoring those tried and true practices and not chasing fads and innovations. You know, introduce the strategy, have students practice, review the work, do more at home, correct that and then move onto the next strategy. Math knowledge builds on itself, skill to skill, so you need to make sure the first is solid before you move..."

"...Onto the next," Gloria interrupted. "I have heard that before."

"I know," Josh said apologetically. "I can get into a rut. But it is about not taking chances that students might miss something. We need to closely monitor what they are doing and how they are understanding it. And math can be great for teaching work habits as you can assign homework nightly. Remember how hard we fought our kids to sit and do their homework every night?"

"Yes," Gloria sighed. "It bordered on the ridiculous. Although, some of the assignments seemed to go on forever. I am still not sure that homework teaches work habits."

Now with a sense of shock on his face, Josh retorts, "What do you mean? How can you not believe that homework helps?"

"Well," Gloria began, "Work habits are not about doing something because you are told to do so. It is about recognizing something needs to be done and then choosing to commit the time to get it done. I found it far more helpful in my business if someone takes initiative and finds a way before I ask them. If I need to ask for everything to be done, nothing will get done. And believe me, I have some very bright people who work for me that need to be told what to do. They did well in school but seem to lack the ability to think for themselves." Gloria stopped chopping tomatoes and began to chuckle. "Remember the assignments that got our kids fired up. The ones that kept them up, excited. They all had a sense of accomplishing something. They were projects and not simply assignments. They were asked to produce something. Tommy even asked us to take him to the library one Sunday afternoon, giving up a Patriot's game, because he was motivated to do well on his defense of wind power as an alternative to oil. He chose he needed to work. That seemed better to me."

"Yeah. But you cannot create those assignments everyday. And skills can get lost inside of them. Students need a well structured curriculum to guarantee they learn the skills. We have been producing great thinkers for generations. Why mess with that tradition?" Josh asked hoping it to be rhetorical but Gloria could not let it go.

"Do you remember when we moved the bake shop in the new direction back in 1991. We thought long and hard about getting rid of the tried and true Sanka and Folgers and bringing in a micro-roaster and a cappuccino machine. We wanted to become a coffee house with great baked goods. Do you remember how the distributor told us it would never work and we should continue to buy the coffee people love and have always wanted? How he told us that people would never adjust their morning routines. People did not want to think in the mornings."

Josh added, "And we were afraid we could lose all of our customer support and the bakery would fail right as our first was entering high school?"

Gloria resumed her point, "Yes. It was a risk. But we decided to do it. And look at what happened. Sometimes being innovative and moving away from the traditional can lead to whole new paths that never seemed to exist. Now there are several micro-roasters in town and I have to say that the coffee is much better."

"I'll say," Josh added. "There is nothing worse then visiting your parents and opening that can of Folgers. Just not the same as a good Fair Trade Arabica bean from Sumatra roasted bold and then brewed with just below boiling temperature. But, we are not brewing coffee. We are working with kids. If we fail, it could be a disaster."

"I would agree," Gloria said reassuringly. "But what is your definition of failure? Are you concerned that you might find a teaching strategy that hits the magic switch inside a student's head and turn their brain off forever? Do you think that if we stopped teaching them in a specific way, we are going to create a bunch of mindless zombies going through life without thinking? No offense, but if all teachers went on strike tomorrow, kids would still continue to think. We don't need to teach kids how to think. Educators are needed to help them think better. More efficiently."

"Yeah. You are right," Josh conceded. "But too often innovative thinking goes awry and the class falls into chaos and then you are left picking up the pieces. It is best to stay traditional."

"I have seen you attempt new strategies only to stop after a few weeks or months," Gloria said.

"Yes. That is what I mean. You try something. The class structure falls apart and you spend the rest of the year trying to reel it back in. Those students have lost almost an entire year by the time you are back to teaching effectively."

"Hogwash," Gloria said sternly. Most likely thinking of another term but would never say it out loud in her kitchen. "You never had a definition for what effective teaching was and you never gave it enough time to be successful. You tried something, it did not go well and you panicked and the easiest thing to do was to head back to the status quo. Do you remember the first few months and then years of the new coffee shop approach. Do you remember some of the old customers writing a petition telling us they would rather buy their coffee from the gas station then to have to purchase our fancy-pants coffee? Do you remember the investment in money it took and how the first few quarters we were actually operating in the red?"

"What's your point," Josh asked more out of frustration because he knew the argument was over.

"My point is simple. Had we not known the vision of what we wanted and the steps to get there, we would have turned around at the first sign of trouble and then most likely been out of business today. Had we not been aware of and willing to lose money the first few quarters, we would have thought we were failures. But we had a vision and we had an ad-hoc metric that was more than the bottom line profits. That allowed us to be innovative and keep the changes alive even as things got difficult."

"Yes but education cannot be run like a business," Josh said sternly in a last ditch effort to draw the argument back.

"I am not saying to run your class like a business," Gloria said with a slight chuckle removing the last bit of energy from Josh's argument. "I am simply saying you can be innovative. That type of thinking is universal. It is also something you should be modeling for your students. If you try something and it does not work when measured against an ad-hoc metric you chose for this innovation, then ask the students if there is something that can improve the strategy and see if it is worth fixing. You have to know what you want to accomplish with the strategy. What would it look and sound like in your classroom if you successfully implemented the strategy. You know, tell the story." Gloria took a quick sip of water signaling to Josh more was to come. "After you know where you want to go, figure out where you are currently. Then figure the steps that are needed to get you to your vision and finally start executing them. Those steps become your ad-hoc measures. You cannot worry about trying to leap to your final destination in a single bound. Measure the steps between to make sure you are moving in the right direction. You can't measure the steps using a metric meant for the end result because you a r e not there yet. Remember how we gave out coupons for free coffee and then measured how many people were returning for more? We lost customers but we knew we were gaining new ones. That is how we knew we were moving towards our vision."

The door bell rang and the door flew open. In marched Kevin with his wife. They were carrying a six pack from one of the local micro-breweries. He tossed one to Josh, gave Gloria a peck on the cheek, and then said, "How about them Yankees?" Josh knew he was still concerned about tomorrow because his reaction was flat. Even though he knew Gloria was correct, he would not be ready to accept the argument that innovation in the classroom was a good thing until he saw it. The good news is, he was about to.

4

Pre-game Strategy

"So. Here we are again. I believe the summers are getting faster," said Kevin as he dipped his chip into the salsa. After only a few chews, he moaned with a sense of satisfaction and said "Dang Gloria. You have outdone yourself this year. This is the best salsa I have ever had."

"Where does the time go," Josh said. "I am not a science guy but is it possible for the world to be speeding up? Maybe we have no way to measure it?"

"Well, I am a science guy," chimed Jim Smits, the science teacher on Alex's new team, "and I have no idea why time passes much too quickly the older you get."

"Well Smitty, now that you are a master teacher, shouldn't you know the answer to everything?" baited Kevin. Jim Smits had thrown himself a party at the end of the last school year to celebrate making it through his fifth year. Being overly superstitious caused him undue stress. He did not want to be one of the fifty percent who burned out and left the teaching profession in their first years. He assumed he was now safe and would remain a teacher for life.

"That is the beauty of science Kevin, there are so many questions still unanswered," Smitty said in a passionate and philosophical tone.

"Sure. Science rules right?" Kevin asked.

"Well it is the reason we need literate and numerate people. If everyone better understood science, we would not elect such ignorant politicians," Smitty said defensively.

"No," Kevin said. "More like if people understood and respected history, we would not repeat the same problems. Have you ever noticed that the reruns of The West Wing are still relevant over a decade later?"

"I believe all subjects are important," Angela said to attempt to switch the conversation. "Besides, you guys should learn from history and end this conversation. It is the same every time you both get together."

Kevin wanted to honor Angela's wishes and change the focus of the discussion. "Time must be getting faster for the new guy, Alex. Have you seen his room. His walls are still bare and he has a bar table in the middle of it. I do not think he will be ready."

"What are you doing about your mentee Josh?" asked Smitty causing all the heads to slowly turn Josh's way.

Josh began to feel nervous but also a little reassured. Maybe his judgment of Alex as a fad chaser was far off and he was simply not ready. He looked at Gloria as if to say 'See. they noticed it too.' He began, "I was in there yesterday and he seemed very calm and together. He was not at all under stress to get the room together. I assume he has a plan for getting it done in time so he just goes about his business."

"Or maybe," Kevin jumped in, "he is so incompetent that he does not even recognize he is behind. He could be one of those that is always behind so it is normal for him. I once heard on NPR how annoying people do not know they are annoying."

"Shocking," said Smitty in a mocking tone.

"Weren't his references stellar?" asked Tess.

"Yes they were," responded Josh with a glance of irritation at Smitty. It was always bad form to share information about a new hire with anyone let alone Tess. Even though she was Smitty's wife, she was not one to be trusted. What Smitty had for a lack of confidence due to the five year burn-out worry, Tess made up for and then some. She has never shied from sharing her opinion on anything. Tess was a high school English teacher, a position she believed made her the most important teacher in the system. It was the pinnacle and in her mind she had the right and the responsibility to help the other teachers better understand what good teaching is.

Smitty's response to Josh's glance was a simple shrug as he averted his eyes as quickly as he could. He knew Tess was like pepper. She added a nice spice to any conversation but could become overpowering very quickly.

"So shouldn't that tell you he is fine and you are all worrying about nothing?" Tess said as she picked up her margarita, which she has to make because no one understands mixology the way she does. She has never said that out loud, but it is clear to anyone who has ever tried.

"Sure. But they could have played him up. You know, get us to take the pint of goods off their hands without looking at the bottom," Kevin said in a joking manner.

"You want to look at his what?" now Tim, Angela's husband was wanting to join the conversation. He was usually quiet, not knowing or caring about school business. But this was fun since it involved something he dealt with regularly as the head of marketing.

"Not his bottom," Kevin jumped in quickly. "I was trying to use a metaphor. You know how they put the bad strawberries on the bottom so you buy the pint only to get home and find some mold? That is what I meant by bottom."

"Oh come on. Administrators don't do that!" Tess responded with such assurance that Kevin felt the challenge. He has not one to back down from such a blatant call-out even when he was not as sure of victory as he was in this one.

"Dale, have you ever given someone a better than deserved reference because you wanted to be rid of them?" Kevin said with a smirk of certain victory.

"You bet." Dale responded without a moment's hesitation nor slowing down his swinging. Dale loved playgrounds and always loved a good swing.

"What?" Tess responded with horror in her voice as though she had just been told that the Pope was not Catholic. "That is unconscionable." A quick sigh was then followed by some fast pants. No one at the table dare speak, nor did they want to disrupt the show, assuming more was to come. "How can you do that? That is against everything that an administrator should do."

"Let me know what you do when you are faced with that dilemma. Until then lets not talk about it." Dale said brushing it aside with such calmness there was nothing left for Tess to do but return to her margarita. Dale threw his hands up and leaped through the air to land on both feet before rolling into a summersault. The children cheered. The adults grimaced.

"One of these days you will break your ankle." said Tim.

"Maybe. But not this day. It is all in how you roll." Dale said as he came to the table, grabbed a beer and smiled at Tess. She attempted to smile back but knew he was right and that bothered her more then the salsa not having cilantro. "I think Alex will be fine. Just give him some time to settle before you pass judgement," Dale said with his fatherly tone. "He just moved across the country and is expecting another child. Just remember he is now one of us and we will support him as he grows. And, I predict, learn something from him. It is all about our professional capital. No one becomes a champion without the right people and personalities around them. Remember the 2011 Red Sox which became the 2012 team. All great superstars, but a lousy team."

The conversation quickly turned to baseball and the defense of the all-time greatest players on the worst teams. Perfect timing for Alex to enter for he was able to quickly discuss the 1984 Chicago Cubs collapse as they fell to the San Diego Padres in the National League Pennant series. He reminded the group how the first baseman let the ball pass right through his legs dashing the hopes of fans who were so anxious for a trip to the World Series. The group decided Alex fit right in, but could he manage it in a classroom. They were about to find out.

5

Opening Day

Josh pulled into the parking lot as the sun began to light the sky. "Red sky at morning, sailors take warning" he thought to himself as he admired the many different shades of colors that streaked the sky. Even though the sky was clear and Jupiter could still be seen, a storm was brewing off the coast and was expected to turn inland by the evening. The geese were already up and flying south in their familiar V-formation. Autumn came early to these parts.

Josh was surprised to see a car in the lot. He had been the first to arrive every day for the past three years. Usually he had time to brew a pot of coffee and have it ready before another would appear. He could see there was a light on in Alex's room. Josh parked his car, entered the building, began the pot, and headed to greet the newest member of the faculty.

Josh was not surprised to see him in so early because he knew Alex still needed to organize his room. As he turned quickly from the hall into Alex's room, he noticed the desks were still in clumps and the walls remained bare. This time he was not able to mask his concern.

"Oh my gosh! Are you going to be ready for kids? You know they come today?" Josh said with panic so thick it made his voice crack.

"Good morning Josh. What was that about my being ready?" Alex said as he removed the ear buds and turned off his iPhone. "I missed what you said. I was listening to some music to get ready for the day. You know, a little pump up mix."

"The students' first day is today." The concern in his voice was still obvious. "You do not really seem ready for them."

"I am," Alex said. "I am very excited. For the first time in my teaching career it feels like the first day of school. In the South, it is hot and humid and we start the first week of August. It was so nice to wake up this morning and feel the crisp, dry, fall air."

Josh did not have time nor interest in small talk. He hasdnever mentored a teacher who did not get off on solid footing to begin the year. Did he let Alex down? Should he have been more supportive and worked with him? He knew his colleagues would give him lip if Alex proved them right by being unprepared. "How can you be ready? Your walls are bare, your desks are in clumps, you have no overhead, I am not even sure where your teacher's desk is. Your room looks like it is being readied to have the rugs shampooed."

"Well, this is how I begin my year. I do not cover my walls as I want to have room to post the students' work from the first few days. They will cover them with the Shared Vision, Code of Conduct, SOP's and Flowcharts. They set their culture," Alex said now feeling confused and slightly embarrassed. This is not how he pictured his first day beginning. Especially not with his mentor.

"What are those things?" Josh snapped in a clearly irritated tone. "The last time I heard of an SOP it referred to how I put the pizza sauce on the dough when I worked for the delivery joint in town."

"Well, it's very similar. SOP's are standard operating procedures for how things happen in my class. Those routines we do to help the class be more efficient."

"How could students possibly know that? They are just getting to your class. How long would it take for them to complete those and leave your walls bare? I mean, isn't it better to tell them and get right into instruction or at least get to know their names?" Josh seemed to be no longer asking but demanding. This caused Alex to flash back to the disappointment expressed by his father when he saw his first apartment. The difference was this time the lack of items was by choice and not economics.

"I should be done by the end of the week with the initial SOP's. You would be surprised at how well students know the typical routines of a classroom. Of course, they have been doing it for eight years and have it pretty set when they get to us."

Josh settled slightly but was still concerned. "The initial. How many will you have?"

Alex smiled now realizing that Josh was concerned that he would lose control of the class. "We begin with the most obvious, like how to turn in papers, how to go to the restroom, sharpen a pencil. You know, the ones we do all the time. Then as those become routine, I will take them down and replace them with new ones."

"How do you know which ones to replace them with and when?"

"Well, I do not know what those are right now. I look for those things students ask over and over again, you know, the ones that make us lose our minds. Then we take the time to create a new SOP for that topic," Alex explained in a tone that was not condescending but informative.

Josh began to switch his weight back and forth from his left foot to his right foot as though he was a second baseman singing the national anthem before game seven of the World Series. "Take time to do an SOP? Seems a better use of time to tell them and make them do it."

Alex smiled and this time responded with a bit more sarcasm then he had been using, "And how has that been working for you? For me, it seems like I repeat the same things over and over and over again. Adolescents have short memories." Alex paused and smiled in an attempt to signal his respect but also his disagreement. He continued, "Besides, I always aim to build a culture of engagement and not a class to manage. Command and control does not teach a single thing. I want students to have a voice in creating their rules. I call the approach Learners Rule."

Josh clearly felt the tone and decided not to push his new teacher any further. He smiled and said, "Of course. I can't wait to see it in action. Seems like a neat idea. I will see you at lunch. Kids are here in about an hour. Good luck." With that he turned and headed for the door. Wanting to say more, maybe even defend his points, but he knew not to rattle the new guy. If Alex was going to struggle, it was going to happen whether Josh stood there and continued pushing or not. The thing Josh could not let go of was the impression that Alex was in complete control.

Alex thanked him for checking in, returned the Earbuds to his ear canal, and continued prepping for the day.

Josh decided to stop by Amanda Hershey's room, another math teacher who started the previous year. He slowly entered the room, cleared his throat so as not to startle her and then smiled when she turned her head towards him.

"Hey Josh. Did you have a good summer?"

"I did. Thanks. How about you?"

"Good," she said. An awkward pause was broken when she finally said, "What can I do for you, Josh?"

He did not know. Why was he in her room? The district had a single year of mentoring and she came along well after a rough start. "I guess I just wanted to see how you were doing." He knew there was more but she would not understand.

"I am great. See. I have my desks in a row. Seating charts are done and my classroom rules are posted on all four walls."

Josh glanced around and sure enough, she had her rules well posted. Nice bulleted lists that included those typical statements of classroom management; No talking without permission, No chewing gum, Be on time, No late assignments accepted. There was very little room for interpretation. The rules stated were for very specific types of behaviors. What happens if a student chooses to do something not on the list?

"I even have my letter ready to go home at the end of the and I have clearly spelled out my late policy. This year there will be no confusion on my expectations. I will state them early and often," Amanda shared with a smile.

"Great," Josh said but he really did not feel as though he meant it. "Let me know if there are any questions or anything I can do to help you. Even though I am no longer your official mentor, I can support you as a colleague."

"I will. Thanks."

"You bet," Josh said while turning and heading to the door. As he exited and started his way down the hall, he said to himself, "See. It is not me. I can mentor. It must be Alex. I can guide people to be prepared and not struggle." He smiled and walked on. The only problem was that he did not feel better. The way Alex defended what he was doing threw Josh. Why did he seem so sure? What can be done to help him? With that Josh paused in the hall. He glanced back to Amanda's room. She had done everything the way Josh taught her and she seemed hopeful she would be able to meet the expectations of the kids. Alex seemed convinced he would as well. With that Josh shook his head attempting to remove the thoughts from his head.

"What's up Josh?," came the voice of the custodian from the far end of the hall. "You alright?"

"Did you hear the thunder, John?" Josh responded hesitantly.

"Nope," John responded in a quick staccato tone. "Sunny as can be out there. Going to be a great day. The storm off the coast will keep everything inside until it turns towards us this evening."

Josh just stood in the hall. "It was so real. I heard it crack."

"Sure you OK Josh?"

"Yeah. I'm good." And he was. The storm he was sensing was not going to take place outside. The storm was going to change him from the inside.

6

The First Pitch

As was customary for a mentor, Josh would watch Alex get settled into his first class. As he left his room and walked down the hall to Alex's he could feel the tension in his chest. A deep breath was very hard to come by. Stressed may be too strong a word to describe the feeling. It was more like slight anxiety. Josh knew that no matter what happened in Alex's class, he was not going to hit "the switch" Gloria referred to and stop the students from thinking. He simply did not want the new teacher to struggle with managing his class and then burn out. He walked in, smiled, and explained to Alex why he was there. Following their previous interaction, Alex was a bit intrigued. Was this typical or was Josh actually worried. "Oh well," Alex thought to himself, "I am confident in what I do." Josh passed the large, circular TGIFridays table, lowered his head in an attempt to deny its existence, and then continued to a seat in the back of the room.

The bell sounded alerting students to make their way down the hall to their first period class. Their faces excited to be back at school but stressed because they did not want to be the first to show it. Alex stepped into the hall, smiled and began to greet students. They moved like a crowd shuffling into a baseball stadium. Instead of holding a ticket and seeking a row number, they used a schedule and the room number. Even if it was not their room it was customary to glance in and see who would not have classes with you. Alex made sure he was visible to all. Even though it was his first day he answered questions and gave directions like a veteran usher at Fenway.

As his students entered the room, he handed them their piece of the cut up calendar that served as their seat assignment.

They looked at him with a "my other teachers never did this" expression. Some verbalized their concerns using that wonderful tone of interested sarcasm that only seems possible from an adolescent. Alex would simply shrug and ask them to figure it out. After the first few students entered and solved the puzzle, they began to help others. Alex loved when this happened. It was a great sign when the community came together and helped each other. He remembered his first principal telling him: "Culture begins at the door on day one. Don't miss it." He never has.

The tardy bell rang. Alex closed the door and with a smile said, "Welcome to your seventh grade math class. I am Mr. Winter." His name always seemed to bring a slight chuckle from the students. He never found it particularly funny when someone's last name was a real word. But then again, many things found humorous to the middle schooler have lost their chuckle factor. Maybe it is maturity, maybe it is experience. He continued the greeting, "I see you all found your seats. Splendid. These will be your seats for now. I will change them from time to time. When that time is depends on what we need done. Sound good?" It was meant as a rhetorical question but Alex also knew that the first day of school was when the students would be the quietest and most attentive. "Let's introduce ourselves to our math community. We will go around the room. When it comes to you, I would like you to stand, say your name, and a strength you bring to this community. We all have them and you need to know what yours is. It does not have to be math related. Before saying it to the whole group, I will give you time to think, then you will share in your table group, and then with the whole community." Alex was cognizant of the importance of having students rehearse in a small group before sharing with the full class. "Any questions?" He paused and glanced around the room. "Alright. If my directions are clear, hold up your five fingers like this." Alex raised his hand high with his fingers spread as though he really wanted to answer a question. "If you are unsure what to do, hold up your fist like this." Now he raised his fist into the air as though he was trying to pump up the team. "If you are sort of confused, hold up the number of fingers that demonstrates how confused. Like, I am sure I know my name and I will share that with my table group, but what does he mean by strength? I might hold up one finger." He turned his head, glanced at a student who Alex already knew to be a leader in classroom disruptions, "Please make sure it is a nice finger." The laughter from the students rose like a wave as they slowly got his meaning. "Okay. On the count of three show me your level of understanding about what we are going to do. One, two, three."

Alex and the students glanced around the room to see who was sure and who needed more support. Alex made a mental note of the few students who flashed the fist. Luckily, every table group had at least one person who was sure what to do. This would give another chance to embed into the culture the idea that we support each other. Without the idea of community responsibility being solid, students who became stuck during project time, would only have a single option for finding help, the teacher.

Alex asked those who were comfortable with the directions to help the others seated at their table. As they began working he set the timer that projected onto his wall and circulated, first visiting those students who showed a fist and then to the others. By the time he met with the first two table groups, the confusion cleared and they were working on communicating their strengths.

After a few minutes, the timer sounded. Alex asked, "Does any group need more time to share with each other? Please hold up the number of fingers for the number of minutes you want." He glanced around the room and said, "I see 1 minute, zero minutes, 2 minutes. Alright, lets do 1 more minute." Alex liked using a timer so the device would become the focus of the students' frustration if they ran out of time.

Josh was amazed at how engaged the students were. He began to reflect on what Alex had done and realized within the first 5 minutes of class the students had needed to figure out how to find their seats, discussed their strengths, supported or got support from their peers, and were preparing to share their strength to the full class. Just then Josh heard the teacher in the next room that shared the wall he was sitting against. The teacher said, "Now that you are in your seats, lets take roll and just confirm who is absent. Please correct me if I mispronounce your name. Simply reply 'here' when I call." Josh thought about how different Alex's opening session was.

When the alarm sounded to indicate the end of the additional minute, he asked for their attention and then modeled sharing his name and a strength. As each student shared, Alex recorded their name and strength on a seating chart. The strengths would come in handy when they encountered frustration during the learning process. Alex always believed you get through something difficult by finding how to use your strength to conquer it. When the material was easy, you used something you want to improve upon. He knew having that level of metacognition was quite sophisticated, but he found the sooner you start practicing the better.

Alex had borrowed this technique from a seminar he attended when he was working as an animal trainer. The exercise was designed to help break down barriers by sharing something you found to be a strength. It also served to let the community know that if you are struggling with a particular concept or skill, you can ask someone who feels they understand it well enough to be considered a strength. As the year went on, they would create many strength charts that allowed students to seek help from each other.

Once all students had an opportunity to introduce themselves and share their strength, Alex asked: "Why are we here?" He liked switching quickly because he could almost imagine the students shaking their heads vigorously to remove the cobwebs.

He could hear their inner-voices, "This fool wants to know why we are here? How long has he been a teacher? Does he not know he teaches us math?"

"Seriously. Anyone know why we are here?" Alex asked again with a slight chuckle.

One student shared rather timidly, "To learn math?" This was Alex's favorite answer. And it was always shared as a question and never a statement. As if students were not sure why school existed.

Learners Rule

"Learning is part of it for sure," he said with a smile to communicate his thanks for taking a risk. After a brief pause he continued, "One thing that is important in any community is to state why we are together. What is the reason we are together. In companies it is often referred to as a shared vision. A statement of why they do business. Think about Walt Disney World. They have often been considered to have one of the best cultures. Everyone in the company has a very clear reason for why they go to work each day. They want to create a wonderful, magical, and memorable experience for all their guests. The Boston Red Sox also have a clear purpose. They want to win baseball games, their division and ultimately the World Series. You would never hear a baseball player say 'we only want to finish third this year.' That would be ludicrous." This brought a slight chuckle from the students. "We need to have that vision for our classroom. This is ,after all, where you come to work." Alex looked and could see the students were listening. It always helps to mention Disney and sports teams. Those are simple examples that connect with many adolescents.

Alex continued with the shared vision prep. "One way companies capture the voice of all their stakeholders, in our case you are the stakeholders of our class, is to ask a question and then have people answer it. It is quick and easy. So, would the person sitting in seat number 2 of your group please come up to the front, retrieve the bin with your table number on it, and take it back to your seat. I will give you 45 seconds to accomplish this. Go."

Alex started his countdown clock that projected on the wall. The students all looked at each other wondering who was in seat 2 and what their table number was. They knew this teacher would not tell them what to do. Soon they began to realize the answer must be somewhere within the room. They simply needed to create the right question and then find what made sense. On one of the walls in the classroom there was a vinyl-adhesive poster, similar to the Colorform toy invented in the 1950s, of the current room arrangement. The table groups were numbered and each seat within the group had a number. The students spotted this and then began to test their ideas. One student rose and headed to the front to get their supplies. When he chose the correct box, Alex glanced up only long enough to smile and then continued shuffling papers in his filing cabinet. This was followed by another and then another until all of the students knew how to solve it. The last student was retrieving their bin when the buzzer sounded.

"Nice job everyone," Alex commented with enthusiasm while the last student made it back to their group. "How did you know who should go and what table you were?"

Silence followed but Alex patiently waited with the slightest hint of a friendly smile on his face. Finally a student spoke. "I watched what he did,"

Alex interrupted, "Do you remember his name?"

"No," the student said while smiling and shrugging her shoulders in a playful way. "He was not in my class last year."

"That's alright," Alex said. "But since we want to form our community, I want you to use names. Since there is not a person on this earth I have met that can remember all names, it is alright to ask for it. Better than calling another person him or her. Simply say, I am sorry, can you share your name with me again? There is nothing wrong with asking. Of course if it is your boyfriend or girlfriend you might be in trouble. But you don't need to worry about that for some time." Alex looked back to the student who began and said, "Let's practice. Again the line is I'm sorry, can you share your name with me again."

The student made the required glances to see if it was alright with her peer group to engage in this bizarre activity. Not seeing anything but giggles, she forged ahead using a tone as though this was the weirdest thing she has ever been asked to do. "I'm sorry, can you share your name with me again?"

The male student told her his name and she continued with her story. "I saw that Jim got up and took table 5's bin. I knew I was in a similar seat so I said to the group I must be seat 2 and we might be table 6. I guess I guessed based on what he, oh I mean Jim did."

Another student now shot her hand in the air seeing an opportunity to share a different successful strategy.

Alex called on her. "Well we used the chart on the wall over there, It looks like the classroom and I could see I was in seat 2 of the group of tables labeled with a 3. So I figured I was in that group, Number 3. I went and grabbed the stuff."

"Well done to you all," Alex said as he stepped towards the chart. "Regardless of the strategy used, either the one by Tess where she watched Jim, or the one by Samantha where she found this chart or one you used that might be different, the fact is you figured out what to do by using clues from the classroom and each other. That is how things will be in here. It is about you and not about me telling you. Don't ask me what the answer is when we are doing full group activities. It is up to you to figure it out. There is not a single right way to solve and sometimes not even a single right answer. You have the power to solve it. Each and every one of you."

Suddenly, the students sat a little straighter in their seats and looked to be more attentive. Alex knew only a single event could have caused such a fast, studious reaction, the principal entered the room from the door at his back. Students knew their teacher's perceived effectiveness depended on how well the students behaved. The difference was Dale did not care if the students were orderly and sitting up straight in their chairs. He was concerned if the students were engaged and could express what the purpose of the lesson was. Orderly classrooms are not always a sign of good learning.

Alex smiled and continued with his lesson. "Mr. Kellogg would you like to join us? We are going to establish a vision for what we are all about in this math classroom?"

Dale said, "Certainly," and walked to a table group that had an open seat. He waved to Josh who was still quietly sitting in the corner with his notebook.

"As I mentioned, we will set our vision to answer one question. That question is WHAT DOES A SUCCESSFUL MIDDLE SCHOOL MATH CLASS LOOK AND SOUND LIKE?" Alex wrote the question on the white board as he said it. "You will write your answers on the stickies in your box. You will write one answer per sticky note and you should write as many answers as you can." He paused, glanced around the room quickly, and then stated, "Give me a fist-to-five on your understanding of what I am asking." Alex wanted to use The Affinity Process because it is easy and a great way to capture the many varied voices of a group.

All of the students held up their hands. Dale gave a curious glance to see what the students were doing. He saw many with all five fingers spread and a few with a fist. Alex also noticed this and said to the students, "Look at the fists. If you are a five, see if you can clear their confusion." He nodded quietly letting them know he wanted it to be done before they move on. After a few moments of conversation he asked again for a fist to five. This time all students shared all five fingers. "This activity begins with you thinking on your own without talking. It is about what you think. No need to put names on your notes. I will be buzzing around to help so if you feel stuck, pop your paw in the air and I will get to you. It is not unusual to run out of ideas before time. But if you sit and reflect quietly, more ideas will seem to float slowly into your mind. Sometimes, those are the best. You just have to wait for them. I will give you 3 minutes to answer the question. Remember, use one sticky per answer but come up with as many answers as you can."

With that Alex turned, set the timer for 3 minutes, and started it. As he turned Dale was standing right behind him. "That was great," he said as though they had just pulled a prank on their best friend. "The students are already working as a group in your class. Before you had told the class to help the students with fists, one young man at my table was already clarifying for his neighbor. What a great community builder. How did you get them there so fast?"

Alex smiled politely and said, "I need to circulate to make sure questions are not setting in. If concerns are not turned into questions they become frustrations. I like to watch for those. If you are interested in the answer to your question I can meet during my planning period. I believe it is block 5."

"Sure," Dale said. "I would love to hear what has happened here. This might be the fastest I have seen this." He opened the door, paused to take one more glance back into the classroom, caught Josh's eyes, shook his head with disbelief, gave him a thumbs-up, and then closed the door behind him.

Alex circulated and made sure there were not any concerns beginning to arise. By the time he finished with Dale, all the students had at least one answer. When the timer sounded, he asked the class if they needed more time. "Please let me know how many more minutes you would like." A few students held up 2 fingers while the majority demonstrated zero in various ways. "Okay one more minute. A compromise. If you feel you have used all your ideas, remember to sit quietly and continue to let thoughts come in. You never know when a good one can hit."

The projected timer counted down to zero and Alex began the next step. "Now, what I need you to do without talking, and I must emphasize without talking, is I want your table to group the words that are similar. Like this," Alex had written four stickies and placed them on his whiteboard. They were 'have homework, fun, bring a pencil, and entertaining.' He did a think aloud as he moved fun and entertaining together. Then he did the same with have homework and bring a pencil. "Are you ready? I will give you 2-minutes."

The students immediately got up and started to work. As Alex had witnessed before, it was really hard for students to begin. They looked around to see what others were doing to make sure they were right. As if they can be wrong. He knows that once they get started with the placement of a single sticky, the dam opens and the trickle becomes a steady flow. Alex looked for the group that was truly stuck. The art of teaching is knowing when the frustration becomes too much. There is a fine line between enabling and supporting. He often wished there was a USDA approved temperature similar to one for chicken or ground beef that indicated how hot the frustration was for each individual student.

The timer sounded. "Now that you have grouped your stickies," Alex announced, "I would like you to label the groups. The good news is now you can talk. In order to label them you may have to regroup some stickies and that is alright. You want your label for the group of stickies to describe all of the actions below them. Remember, you cannot do this wrong, so simply decide what word or phrase works."

Students struggled at first to understand what he meant. But they were already getting used to the fact that this teacher did not give them the answer. Alex knew there was not a single right answer to this activity. In fact, the more outside the lines they think, often the better the group work is. Even if they wrote group names that were completely unrelated, they would learn. The work expended to understand something, is where the heart of true thinking lies. If he solved it for them and they simply wrote his guided answer on a piece of paper, they have not learned a thing except how to be a scribe. Alex wanted more from his students.

Alex glanced at the clock and realized he needed to interrupt the conversations, something he always hated to do. "We only have 5 minutes left of class and we need to wrap-up the day."

"Man. That was a fast class period," a student was overheard saying. "I don't think an hour class has ever passed that quickly."

Alex began, "I like to finish everyday with a self-reflection of how you did today. That is why you have your notebooks. Please take them out." He paused for a moment and then continued. "Please put today's date at the top of the page. Each journal entry needs a date. Typically we will review how you did working towards the goal you set for yourself. You will reflect on what you did, what obstacles stand before you and what will happen tomorrow. You can also keep track of things that went well, what you liked or what you did not. That way you will begin to know yourself as a learner. That will be critical as you get older. Helps you find a job you like. Don't worry too much about what I just said. We will create an SOP for reflection writing either tomorrow or the next day."

"What did he call us?" asked a student to another in the back. "Did he say SOB. I have heard my mother call my father that when she is not too happy."

"My mother says worse," the other student responded while rolling his eyes.

Alex overheard so tried quickly to refocus the boys. "No," chuckling at their conversation, "SOP. Stands for standard operating procedure. We will discuss more tomorrow. Today, I ask that you simply reflect on how you felt about today. Also, what is the biggest struggle you have had in math. Struggle does not mean you do not understand it now. 3 minutes. I will collect your charts as you work."

Alex circled the room and collected the charts. Occasionally he would stop to comment on what someone had written. The students enjoyed the direct contact with their new teacher. As the timer came to 10 seconds left, Alex asked the students to close their journals, grab their stuff and head to their next class. "Thanks so much for a wonderful day. Enjoy your night." He placed the charts on his back shelves with a sticky labeling first period and headed to the door. It was time to greet the next class with the cut-up calendar and repeat the process. Josh walked by him, patted him on the shoulder, and headed into the hallway. Alex could see that the notebook Josh had was blank. Why he wondered. Was what I did not that memorable?

After the first few weeks, when the students were settled into their work, the days would become less routine. All the time spent building a culture of independent learners would pay off. Alex was a firm believer in students working at their academic readiness level. You cannot truly differentiate if students are reliant on the teacher as the sole source for routine questions. He enjoyed being available to help students work through sticky points in their learning and letting them be responsible for finding a pencil. Unfortunately the great feelings of the first successful class would fade. No one could have predicted how soon.

7

The Code

The second day of school began in the same sequence as the first. Josh made his way into the parking lot and saw Alex was already in his classroom preparing for the day. "Why?" Josh thought to himself. "He did not do anything but have the students answer a question. How much planning could that require." Josh made the coffee and went straight to his room without stopping by Alex's. Josh would come to realize it was not out of rudeness, he simply knew he had nothing to say about what he witnessed yesterday and was afraid Alex would ask.

The bell rang and the students marched through the hall to their rooms. Teachers were still present to help those students who need a reminder to get to first period. As the halls emptied, Josh could feel the hormones of anxiety seep through his entire body. He knew he needed to go back into Alex's classroom. He had no idea why he was anxious. Maybe because in all his years of teaching, he had no suggestions for his new mentee. Maybe because Alex was already firing on all cylinders, he had guilt over taking money to mentor.

"What would be the big deal if I did not go? Would anyone even notice? Then I would really not be earning my money." Josh said as he was about to enter the room.

"Hearing thunder again Josh or simply talking to yourself," came the familiar gruff of the janitor.

"Nope, John. Just talking to myself," Josh said as he took a deep breath, tucked his still empty notebook under his arm, and opened the door as he gave himself a little pep talk. "You can do this."

"Curiouser and Curiouser," the janitor said as he continued sweeping the leaves the students transported in from the parking lot.

Josh entered the room, made eye contact with Alex, lifted his head to greet him, and then went to the same seat in the back of the room. Josh could hear the low roar of the students and assumed Alex had not yet started the class. It was only 2 minutes after the bell but Josh had written two sentences in his notebook to remind him to tell Alex about the importance of starting class right away. The first ten minutes of each class period is when the mind is most awake and able to take in new information. Josh was momentarily pleased that he had something to share when he noticed the conversations were less about playful things and more about what happened yesterday. Josh saw an open seat at a group and went to sit with them. "What are you working on?" Josh asked the group of students.

One of the students pointed to the whiteboard and read what was written, "With your group, reflect what we did yesterday and why we did it. Be prepared to share with the whole class."

"Do you mind if I listen?" Josh asked the students. Only the student trapped in Josh's gaze when the question ended felt the need to respond with a simple shrug. Josh knew he would need to get them going again as is typical when an adult joins any conversation. "So what did you say?"

"Well we talked about why we are here, you know, why we come to school," said one of the three female students in the group.

"And we talked about Disney and stuff. He even mentioned the Red Sox," said the only male.

"Yes," said the female again, "but those were examples and not what we did. I think he wants to know why it was important."

Another student nodded and then chimed in, "True, but it does help to have the examples. It made me recall better. I love Disney."

"And why we did it was so we know the purpose for coming to the classroom," said the male student. "You know, we are here to learn but that is too simple. Just like the Red Sox are not about winning games. They are about winning games to win the World Series. Anything short is not good enough. So we are here to learn but we are also here to work together to win the World Series of our lives."

The last statement was delivered with sarcasm so if thought weird or wrong by the other students, the student's ego would be protected. But Josh, being the quality educator he was saw it as an opportunity to push deeper. "Tell me what is the World Series of your life?"

Josh was surprised how quickly the students answered, "You know, we are not here to simply learn today. We are preparing ourselves for being successful when we finish with school."

Another of the female students jumped in. "I think Mr. Winter wants us to not only get good grades, which is like winning games, but he also wants us to be in a place that helps us grow in a professional sense. You know. It is hard to say since I have not worked in a place like Disney, but a job is not just a job if it is what you do for your life." She began to look away and shake her head. "I don't know what I am saying."

"Yes you do. That was awesome," came a voice from over her shoulder. As she spun she saw it was Mr. Winter. "That was a really nice way to say it. You do not need to be an adult working in an adult job to understand the importance of knowing why you are doing something." Alex turned and moved to another table.

Josh smiled at the students and asked, "Did you like this activity."

"I guess so," said the male student. "I have never had a teacher ask me why I thought I was in school or his class. It was nice to talk about why we come to school. Usually I sit here and listen to why the teacher tells me I am here. My parents also thought it was a nice idea."

"I wish other teachers would do this. Some need to do it for themselves. I think they have forgotten why they are in school," said the female student who started the conversation. "It was as if school was about us and not about what needs to be done. You know what I mean."

Josh was beginning to get the picture.

The timer ran down and Alex turned and addressed the class, "Alright, I heard some great conversations. I would ask for two groups to volunteer their thoughts with the whole group."

The groups shared and it was easy for Josh to see they had similar thoughts and got the point of the lesson. Alex summarized the lesson from yesterday once again reiterating that this classroom would be about a community and about working together to get done what we need to get done. "Learning should not be something done to you but a tool that you can use to help you understand how the world works. I am not worried about teaching you. I am worried about what you have learned. You cannot learn if you are not an active member of the community. So we need to vote on our vision statement. I will read it and then we will vote using our thumbs. Up if it is good. Down if you want it changed. Everyone gets one vote and you must vote. Ready?" He unrolled the chart paper that was taped on the whiteboard. He read the statement, "We are learners, in control of our actions, engaged to grow, and applying knowledge so we care." Alex paused a few moments to allow for the students to think. As he looked at the class he realized he needs to allow them time to process out loud with each other. After all, learning is social. "Please take a moment at your tables to discuss if this statement captures what was discussed at your table yesterday. 3 minutes."

When the timer sounded, Alex simply asked the students to vote. All gave a thumbs-up. The shared vision was accepted. "Once the other classes have voted, we will hang our vision in the front of the room. It is so important to know why we are here. It is also important to know how we will act. So with that, we will create our Code of Conduct this morning." Alex loved keeping a quick tempo, especially to open the year. "We will think around how we will act within our community to ensure learning for all." Alex paused, smiled and then turned on his LCD projector. "Our school created a school-wide code that is displayed on posters and hung throughout the building. You have probably seen these." As Alex spoke he showed slides of the different posters. Josh was stunned that Alex was already aware of them. He wondered how many of his colleagues who were here when the School-wide Behavior Code was created even know the posters existed. "Our positive behavior expectations are ready, respectful, responsible. As you see here in the cafeteria each of the terms have different descriptors underneath them. The ones in the restroom have different descriptors under them. As one would hope, you know that being ready, respectful, and responsible in the cafe should be different then the bathroom. The rooms have two totally different purposes. True the actions in one room often cause the actions in the other, but you do not want to get them confused." The students shook their heads showing disapproval but Alex knew that was adolescent speak for 'I am listening'. "So we are going to take the words, ready, respectful and responsible, and identify words and phrases that work in our classroom. What I want is for table groups 1 and 2 to work together on Ready. Table 3 and 4 you will have Respectful and 5 and 6 will take Responsible. I want person in seat 3 of the odd group to record the words or phrases that you would use to say a person was acting respectful or responsible or ready in our class. How you answer depends on the word you have. Any questions. Lets do the fist to five." As happened yesterday, many were five but there were some fists. "Alright fivers, please help those who are fists. I believe we have enough who know what to do so we can proceed. Remember, there is no wrong way to do this. Don't get stressed, just try something. Five minutes. Go."

The students began chatting while the student in seat three took out his pencil and began recording the thoughts of the group. Josh could not believe this all happened in the first 10 minutes of class. How could he get through all of this so quickly? He jotted a note so he would remember to investigate.

When the five minutes had passed, the students shared their thoughts. Alex created a master list for each of the three focus areas on chart paper and hung them in the front of the room.

"As you can see, we have too many expectations to remember," Alex said as he pointed to the signs. "We need to narrow. How about under ready we say.." He continued until he had word smithed the code to have three to five phrases under each or the focus areas Ready, Respectful, Responsible. "Now we are going to vote to accept. This time however, I want you to feel free to express yourself without fear of being seen by others. We will use a process called Secret Acceptance Chart. As you can see on this chart there are four quadrants, just like you might remember from graphing. You are going to use dots to vote for how you feel about our Code of Conduct. Along the bottom, labeling the x-axis, you can see the words 'I think the Code is fair'. If you think the Code is really fair you want your dot to be far to the right, in this quadrant. If you think it is not fair, you want it to the left side of the paper. Going up and down, labeling the y-axis, you see the words 'I can live to the Code'. This is asking if you think the Code is something that you can do everyday in our class. If you think you can be these things on the paper listed under Ready, Respectful, Responsible, then you would put your dot towards the top of the paper. If you feel the expectations are something you would really struggle to meet on a daily basis or are unfair, you would put your dot towards the bottom. If you are not all the way to either side, then put your dot on the paper where you think it best represents you." Alex knew this was quite a complex task, but he believed in challenging them early, before they settled into their passive reliance on the teacher. "Let me show you an example." He drew four quadrants on the board. Along the horizontal axis he wrote 'I like baseball'. Along the vertical axis he wrote 'I like Boston Sports Teams'. "Okay, Lets say I was a Red Sox fan, where would I put my dot? Discuss with your table groups." Alex allowed about 30 seconds and then called the group back. He did not use the timer with the quick Turn and Talks because he wanted to preserve its effectiveness for the longer conversations. "Alex rolled a set of dice. Alright, table 4 seat 3, where should it go." The students all glanced at each other wondering what the dice had told him. Alex used the blue die for the table group and the red die for the seat number. This was a cheap alternative to a random number generator.

"We thought it would be in the upper right of the graph," said a student with that lack of certainty that is unfortunately prevalent in many learners.

Alex glanced at the chart and then back to the student. "Why?"

The student shifted in his seat and glanced down at his desk. Then raising his head he said "Well, if you are a Red Sox fan, that means you must like baseball a lot and they play in Boston. That would mean you are quite positive in both squares."

Alex smiled. "Yes you are right." He placed the dot on the board. "As Tim said, since baseball is my thing and the Sox play in Boston I would put my dot in the furthest corner of this quadrant." Glancing at Tim he said, "That is what these square things are called. Quadrants." He turned his body to face the class again and said "Okay, how about a Yankees fan? At your tables."

This continued until the students had a sense of how the Acceptance Chart worked. Alex gave them time to think about where they would put their dot and then had them line up and vote with their dot. The chart was turned toward one corner so the others could not see how someone had voted. The students had red, blue and yellow dots. Alex placed some green dots on the chart so the first few voters were still anonymous. Only Alex knew the green dots did not matter. After all had voted, the chart was turned toward the class and the students discussed what the distribution meant. With five minutes left in class, Alex had the students take out their journals and begin reflecting on how the day had gone. Josh looked over the shoulder of one of the students who had graciously included him in the activities. The student expressed how he felt valued for being included in shaping how the class worked. Another student also expressed hope that the class would be able to meet the expectations as she believed it would be an environment that would allow her to learn. Josh closed his notebook, stood, and began heading toward the door. This time he paused at Alex's barroom table, patted him on the shoulder, and said "impressive." The buzzer sounded and the students grabbed their stuff and followed Josh out of the door. Alex smiled and wished them all a wonderful Wednesday.

8

High and Inside

Alex could hear his stomach growl. The giggles of the students sitting closest to him informed him it was loud. "I am hungry too. When is lunch?" asked a student in the back of class.

'Wow, Was my stomach that loud,' Alex thought as he checked his bell schedule and then glanced at the clock to make sure he did not make a mistake. Realizing he still had a minute, he checked the timer, saw it had thirty seconds, so he asked the students to close their journals.

The students slowly exited the classroom all a murmur about what today's lunch would be. Regardless of how good the food actually was at the school, the students always made the same disparaging remarks. Alex shut the door behind the last student and headed down the hall to the teacher's lounge.

As he entered, one of the teachers caught his eye and smiled. "How are you adjusting? Still surviving?"

"Yes. Thank you," Alex responded. Getting tired of the same comments from the same people. Even though it was the end of the first week he responded using the same phrase, "The students are great. So polite and eager. I love opening days."

"Just wait," said the voice from the corner. That was new ,thought Alex. As he turned he saw a teacher who had nestled himself into a corner. Alex was not even sure how he could fit. Not that he was too large, although he did have an impressive frame. He had both shoulders and hips in contact with the two perpendicular walls that made the 90 degree corner. No human was going to come between him and the wall. He seemed like a cornered raccoon, although Alex could not see a vicious snarl. The teacher glanced up from his lunch and continued, "They will not stay that way. I have been doing this for thirty-five years. It is always the same. They rise up by October and then teaching them becomes a battle of the wills."

"Oh pipe down George. You have been saying that since the first day we started together and it was twenty-five years ago." Alex turned his neck to see a woman standing at the door. She looked too young to be teaching for so long. Most likely a result of her positive spirit. "Don't listen to old George. He came in that way." She grabbed a sandwich from the fridge and then sat opposite George.

Alex saw his team so walked over to sit with them. "Hey guys," Alex said while taking an open seat at the table.

"Hey Alex," said Kelly, the English teacher on his team. "How is the first Friday? I hope you are enjoying our school. Do you have any questions?"

"The students have been great. I find them to be very interested and excited about being at school."

"Yeah?" said Jim Smits, the team's science teacher. The comment was made with such a thick slab of sarcasm it was as though someone dropped a rock right on the table. "The students, who have always sat politely and listened to me read the rules and procedures of a proper science lab, wondered if we were going to talk about what a good science student is like. You know as they did in Mr. Winter's class." The comment was made while he simultaneously rolled his eyes and looked at the others at the table in an attempt to suck them into his complaint. "What is that all about," he finished with a teasing tone.

Alex was not sure if he should take Smitty's comments as an assault or as from someone who was simply trying to make conversation in a socially awkward way. Kelly was not wondering. She felt it was too strong for the first lunch. "Smitty, I feel you are coming on a little strong. Are you that upset about what the students asked?"

"No," said Smitty while attempting to be shocked, "I just wanted to know what was happening in Alex's classroom that got the students buzzing."

Alex smiled and shared how he was using an affinity process to capture the students' thoughts on what a successful classroom looks and sounds like. Groups of students gave categories that he then organized into a statement that was voted on and accepted by the students. Alex continued explaining how he created the Code of Conduct. That was when the cork came out of the bottle.

"That is ridiculous." Smitty said. This time without the faintest attempt to hide his disagreement. "Students need to be told what the rules are. How can we let them decide? Who runs this place, the students or the adults? Do we really want them to believe that students rule?"

"Well, I did not give them the control of my classroom, let alone the school. I simply wanted them to think about what a good classroom could be."

"How can they possibly know? They just got here," Smitty said while flashing Alex a look that screamed "Duh!"

"Well I believe it is important to let the students have a strong voice in their classroom. You know, let them weigh-in before they buy-in."

"They have nothing to buy in to!" Smitty was beginning to show his frustration. "They need to do what I tell them to do. I cannot have a science class that decides we do not need to be careful with glass test tubes and chemicals."

Alex smiled. Realizing Smitty was feeling threatened by something he was doing, he tried to shift the conversation. "Of course not. It is not about safety procedures like you must face in your labs. It is about how we vision our learning environment. Why are we here. And also how we will act to meet our vision."

Smitty was now grinning, "Oh I get it. You want a community of learners instead of a classroom of students. "

Alex grinned, "Yes. I guess that is a way to say it."

"Well I think students have been entering schools for 100 plus years, sitting in rows, and learning without asking for their buy-in," Smitty said while making air quotation marks around the word buy-in.

"I think we need to simply teach these students," came a voice from another table.

'Who said that,' Alex wondered as he glanced to see George. Having finished his burrito, he was now ready to join the conversation. "I have seen many things come and go around here and at the end of the day, we always return to having students comply with the classroom rules. You know. Do what we say. That prevents anarchy and teaches responsibility"

"What is wrong with that?" asked another voice. Alex did not know this teacher's voice. As he glanced to politely make eye contact, he was stunned by the striking resemblance to Alice from the Brady Bunch. She was even wearing a pale blue shirt. Luckily, he was able to refrain from bursting out loud or asking about Sam the Butcher.

"Yeah," Smitty said with emphasis. "What is wrong with having students 'Buy in' to the vision I tell them?"

Alex was now very uncomfortable. He realized that he had not even taken a bite of the sandwich his wife had made for him to celebrate the first Friday. He began to shift in his seat hoping any of the 15 teachers in the room would change the subject. But they did not. He could feel all eyes were locked and watching him.

"I do not like it when new teachers come in here with some wild, outside ideas and try to think we all need to change," said the Maid Alice look alike.

"That is not what I am doing," Alex said, his voice slightly trembling with defensiveness. "I just like to run my classroom this way."

"That is all well and good," Smitty said with a false sense of relief. "You keep it in your classroom. The only problem I have is how it affects our team."

"Well," smiled Kelly, "I have not had students wondering about how we are going to run our ELA class. Maybe you are too controlling, Smitty. You know how many times I have told you that you needed to relax and remember they are adolescents and not young scientists."

"You know, it's best to simply ignore the students and do what you wanted to do and make them learn it," said Stan Schram, the social studies teacher on Alex's new team. He was advertised as a man of few words but he finally decided he needed to say something. "If I stopped each time a student asked me to do something differently or wanted to take me in a different direction, I would never be able to cover my content."

"I try," Smitty said in a defensive tone. "They can be so persistent and distracting."

"Not if you remember who the expert is in the room," Stan said with authority, like a father giving his son a pep talk as he prepares for a promotion at work.

"Yeah. How do you plan to control them?" Smitty said, now feeling the confidence of having all of the teachers in the room agreeing with him. "I think you are setting yourself up for disaster in October. I think George is right. They do seem to turn and if you don't have control, you will lose the ability to teach. And then our team will be the team no one wants."

"You make an assumption I will lose control," Alex shot back leaving anyone listening to know he has had it with the conversation.

"We shall see. But I am not feeling good about it. I hope for your sake you can control the class," Stan said with a smile as he began to clean up his area. It was clear that he thought he was right and enjoyed getting the final word.

"I just hope it does not infect our team," said Smitty still showing signs of worry. "I finally made it to the five year cliff, I am not interested in having anything burn me out."

"Have a great weekend everyone," Maid Alice said as she stepped into the now busy hallway.

"Come on boys. Time to head back. I can hear our students in the hall," Kelly said. She stood up, patted Alex on the shoulder and said, "Don't let them get to you."

As much as Alex appreciated Kelly's words he never understood why people said not to worry. If you knew their words were bothersome, why would they not bother him. Alex collected his sandwich and wrapped it back up, hoping he would have time during his prep period to actually eat it. Maybe his appetite would return.

'Wow,' he thought to himself and then took a deep breath, 'this is going to be a long year if this is what lunch will be like.' He grabbed a paper towel, ran it under some cold water, and wiped his face. 'I like to think of them as learners and not simply students. And I am not interested in the learners ruling the school. Why does it boil down to who is in control. Ruling is not controlling by default. The people rule in a democracy through representation. To think learners cannot be part of the decision on the rules because they will have too much control, sounds more like a totalitarian approach to leading. We want them to understand they have a voice in the rules that will govern their lives. After all, they will be future leaders of our country,' he thought to himself as the heat in his face was cooled by the towel. He turned and opened the door to the teacher's lounge and had a feeling that caused him to glance back to the lunch tables. It was then that he noticed a single figure who had remained seated at a table that was blocked from Alex's view during lunch. It was as if this person had chosen to sit in a secret alcove in a night club to eaves drop on an unfaithful spouse. Now the mystery person was simply staring back at him. Once Alex was able to identify him his heart sank as the feeling of betrayal swept over him. It was Josh. How could he not say anything to defend him? He was in my class. Was the class so awful that he did not have a reason to share what he saw? Even if it was to simply change the focus of the inquiry and give him a break. Alex sighed, dropped his head and then turned slowly back toward his classroom. Much of his enthusiasm and excitement was gone. Not feelings of failure or disappointment. He just felt as though the good credit he built in his emotional bank had been depleted.

"Hey Mr. Winter," shouted some students as they moved down the hall. "A bunch of us were talking at lunch that we should do a code for what the cafeteria should look and sound like. You weren't here last year but it was bad. Loud, messy, out of control. Students cut the lines and even threw food. The lunch ladies got so mad they gave us all assigned seats. I hated that. I like to sit with my friends during lunch. If we did that thing you showed us, we think more people will care since it would be our vision of the cafe and not the control of the evil lunch lady."

Alex always wondered why certain positions in schools always had the same reputation. The lunch people he had worked with were always so nice, but the students were all afraid of them. Even librarians seemed to get a certain reputation that was not accurate. He began to answer the student, "Yes. It could work. I would talk with Principal Kellogg and see if that is something he would support. I would be more than happy to help, but it needs principal approval first." Alex turned into his room. "Have a great afternoon."

"Yeah. You too. Thanks, Mr. Winter. I love your class."

Alex turned on his lights and stood at the door a moment. "That is why I do what I do. I want students to begin to see they have some control. Maybe Kelly was right. I should not let them get to me." He glanced at the sign he always keeps posted on the inside wall of his desk where his chair tucks under. "Illegitimi non carborundum est." He smiled realizing that would not be the last time he would have that thought.

9

Coaches Reflection

"I don't think you understand. I just sat there. I did not speak up. I could have stopped it," Josh said with a snap.

"Please do not yell at me," said Gloria. "I know you are frustrated, but it is certainly not at me."

"You are right." Josh said while hanging his head in a submissive posture looking for forgiveness. "It's just that I did not do what a good mentor should do, protect the new teammate from the spoils of the others. Can you imagine if a veteran catcher did not defend his new pitcher. I just let the others feed on him."

"How bad was it?" Gloria asked.

"Well, nothing unexpected if you know their personalities. They are all great teachers but can be very opinionated. And they become overwhelmed when they hear about something new. Alex's approach is different. Simple, but different. It makes me think of that book we listened to together last year. Switch, I believe it was, by Dan and Chip Heath. You know, what looks like resistance is a lack of clarity. They are simply unclear. They always vent first and then they investigate. Once they know what is being discussed, they will knock it out of the park. But if you do not know them, you can take their opinions and ventings as insults," Josh said.

"Well, my feeling is, regardless of intent, if your words and actions cause another to feel attacked, then you are not acting as a supportive teammate," Gloria said emphasizing supportive.

"Yes. That is the problem. I am sure Alex felt awful. I could hear it in his voice but I could not say anything. I just sat there and watched as he was questioned by the others. He did not even get to eat his sandwich. I know how much he loves sandwiches. And it was Meg's First Friday Sandwich.

"What?" said Gloria with a puzzled look on her face. "How do you know about Meg's sandwich making skills?"

"One of those strange facts you remember from a conversation," Josh said.

Gloria moaned and made a sad face indicating her sorrow felt for Alex.

"I am not looking forward to going back into his room Monday morning," Josh said while he stood to clear the dinner table.

"What?" Gloria shouted, as though a knife was sliding from the plate and about to stab Josh's foot causing him to pause momentarily. "You were in his room this morning?"

"Yes. It is customary for mentors to be in the rooms during their planning periods the first few days. I usually spend the first week or so."

"So how bad was it?" Gloria said slowly and deliberately so not a word was missed. She was afraid of the answer.

"Actually, it was amazing. Absolutely flawless. He had all the students engaged in taking control of the classroom. They had an authentic voice," Josh began describing with so much enthusiasm it caused Gloria to begin to smile. He continued, "On the first day he had the students describe why they are there. Why are they coming to class. He called it the Class Shared Vision. Then he had the students create a Code of Conduct using the words from the school-wide discipline code, Ready, Respectful, Responsible. I sat at a group and listened and watched as these seventh graders talked about what a respectful math class would look and sound like. They had so many wonderful ideas. Even better then some of mine. They seemed so enthusiastic and proud of what they created. He then had them vote to not only accept it but if they felt it was fair and if they could meet the expectations of the code. It was a..." Josh made eye contact with Gloria. "What are you smiling at"

"Well, it is the excitement and enthusiasm on your face. You truly seemed as though you enjoyed it."

"I did." Josh said humbly. "The simplicity and the effectiveness of it was masterful. It was like an All-Star swing." Then Josh's face shifted, losing some of the enthusiasm. "But then I did nothing to defend him. I have never really witnessed that kind of community building in a classroom. I was not sure what to say to defend him. And I was not interested in having their anger turned towards me. And you know, all the stuff he did is stuff I have heard about and tried myself. But he did it with such, ah," struggling to find the words, Josh looked to the light for a moment. His gazed snapped back and he confidently said, "poise." His face immediately crumpled. "Well it sounded better in my head and less about describing a dancer. But I do believe that is the word I am looking for. His transitions from activity to discussion to activity to processing was seamless. He never spoke for long. It was all about the students working. He was very well scripted but it just flowed. You would think he had 20 years of experience."

Gloria decided to throw out the question, "So what are you going to do about letting him hang there?"

Josh dropped his head at the shoulders and let it bounce a bit and then answered, "Oh yeah. I almost forgot. Boy, if only you could have seen his face. He seemed like Mel Gibson in Braveheart. You know the scene when he discovers that one of the attackers is Robert the Bruce. Man. What a let down."

Gloria laughed, "You know not everyone can quote that movie?"

"Pity. People should. There is only one thing to do. I must see him first thing Monday morning and let him know I would like to talk about why he does what he does. That way I can be better prepared to defend what is happening. Maybe even help others do it."

"That is a very nice way to approach it. I wish I had a mentor who has enough respect for what I am doing and also enough courage to admit they do not know what I am doing so they ask me about it," Gloria said with a smile of support.

"Well," Josh said, "That's the thing. I don't think I am his mentor. I believe the roles are switching."

Josh finished the dishes, gave Gloria a kiss on the cheek and headed to the couch to watch a few innings of the Red Sox before he headed to bed. Josh liked this time of the season because he could watch the September call-ups get a chance to play in the big leagues. When the television picture became clear, Josh could see the veteran catcher was on the mound talking with the 21 year old pitcher who was one of the top rated prospects in the Red Sox organization. Often Josh wondered what crafty bits of wisdom the veteran postulated to the new meat. But on this evening, Josh began to wonder if the prospect had something to say to the catcher that might improve his game.

10

A New Way to Throw

Monday morning was clear and bright with a simple chill in the air. The smell of people firing up their wood stoves in an attempt to bring the indoor temperature to an appropriate sixty-five degrees, hung in the valleys. Josh knew if he was to establish and maintain a supportive relationship, he would need to face Alex today and have a crucial conservation. He and Gloria had read a book during their marriage counseling about how to have a dialogue and make it safe for the other to receive feedback and share their thoughts. They went to counseling to see if there was more to gain from their relationship and not because of any specific problems. It was Josh's idea of course. He had not been presented with a chance to practice using the conversation skills he learned. This was his moment. He started the coffee, waited for it to finish brewing, grabbed the pot, and headed to Alex's room.

"Good morning Alex," Josh said as he handed a cup of coffee to Alex who was seated at his high table looking at his computer. Josh could see he had the Red Sox website up.

"Good morning Josh," Alex said with a bit of surprise. "I was trying to catch up on the Red Sox so I can talk about last night's game with students. As much as I love baseball, we do not have cable yet so watching games is not a possibility. Seems as though they have a good team this year. That young pitcher seemed remarkable last night."

Josh could barely hold his enthusiasm. "Yes. I was able to watch. It was amazing. They say he has a whole new way to throw. Not sure what that means. Baseball has been a professional sport for well over a hundred years. How does someone all of sudden develop a new way to throw? I did not see it as I watched. Seemed the same to me."

"Probably depends on the perspective with which you observe him. From the fans it looks the same. From the hitter's view, it is like nothing they have ever seen," Alex said. "The expert hitters expect one thing and he has found a way to disrupt that stimulus-response chain and surprise them. Sometimes surprises are good and sometimes they are not. Again, that is a matter of perspective."

Josh sat for a moment and realized a thought was beginning to stir but he was not quite sure what it was. He shrugged it off and said, "I need to come out and say something. It is not easy but I want it out and then we can move forward." Alex's eyes widened and he pulled his shoulders back slightly to communicate his worry about what Josh was about to say. "Friday in the lunchroom, when the other teachers were interrogating you about how you run your class, I did not come to your defense."

"You do not need to defend me," Alex said in a tone meant to relieve Josh of his concern.

"No. I really did. It was unfair. Even though the teachers here are very supportive, they do get concerned about what they do not understand. We are a fairly traditional community and the traditional structure is for the teacher to control the classroom through strong management. The fact that you were asking the students to create why they are here and how they should behave, caused them to ask the other teachers to do the same."

Alex jumped in, "That was never my intention. I was simply being true to the teacher I am and how I want my class to run."

Josh smiled, "I know that. I was here. They were not. They are simply responding to the students asking them to change. It is not easy to change habits let alone when the students are asking for it."

Alex smiled back, "I know. It also can make someone feel like what they do is not appreciated. All teachers want students to think of them and their class as their favorite. Even if we do not admit it, we like to have our students excited and engaged. "

"Ain't that the truth. Even million dollar athletes feel the sting of the boo-birds that can rain down after a disappointing performance. Why would teachers be any different?" Josh asked.

"I tried the authoritarian class management style. I wound up losing control of my class by mid-October because it was not who I was and the students saw right through it, " Alex attempted to explain, almost sounding defensive.

"Yeah. Dang adolescents. Once they sense lack of authenticity they can pounce. I have been there myself."

"Right," Alex said. "But you do not need to explain the others."

"Well," Josh interrupted, "as your mentor I should have done a better job of explaining myself. Quite frankly, I was not sure what I witnessed in your room the last week. It was so smooth, it was hard to tell where the work was. It was so graceful"

Alex laughed, "Not sure what to say. I simply plan to let my kids do as much as they can. My job is to create those opportunities for them to think and then let them go."

"I am here this morning to pick your brain. I want to know why you did what you did. I know from all my years of coaching that what seems effortless usually has years of deliberate practice hidden underneath. No one simply is. They have an approach that is supported with hard work and a solid philosophy. I want to be that catcher who is supporting the kid with the new way to throw. But I cannot do that unless I understand what I saw. It was one of the best approaches to community building I have ever witnessed. The second day, the students were already supporting each other. If someone was stuck, another student would step in without hesitation and show them how to do it. I know that was not an accidental happening. You made specific decisions to create that environment. I have tried to do that over the years without much success. You got it. I want to know what you were thinking so I can help other teachers see why what you do works."

"Wow," Alex said with an overpowering humility. "That is really nice of you to say but.."

Josh interrupted him. "I do not have time for you to pretend that it was not amazing and then I tell you it is and we go back and forth until we agree to just accept the compliment. So, just accept it. I really enjoyed it."

"Thanks," Alex said accepting the compliment. "I am not sure where to begin. I guess I can tell you what I used to do and why I now do what I do."

"That would be great. We still have an hour or so until the students arrive. If we need to pause and pick it up another time we can. But let's get started."

Alex smiled, "I have never explained my thinking on creating a classroom culture before, so it might be a bit choppy. Please stop me at any point and ask for clarification or if there is something specific you want to hear about, just ask."

"Okay. Got it. Glad I brought the pot of coffee in this morning," Josh said as he topped off both cups. He took out a note pad and wrote "Classroom Culture" across the top. "Maybe begin with why you call it Classroom Culture."

Alex stepped off of his raised seat and begin to pace slowly. Clearly a thinker who needs to be moving in order to process. "When I started teaching I was under the impression that you must not give them an inch or they will take a mile. I had not been around adolescents or any student for that matter, since I was one myself. I thought I needed to control the classroom. You know, teach the students how to mind."

"I am guessing by the way you are phrasing it and your tone of voice that did not really work for you," Josh said chuckling.

"No. It really didn't," Alex said smiling back. "The students quickly learned that was not my personality so I had a hard time remembering what I wanted to accomplish with my discipline. But I did not give it up. I visited other classrooms and saw a range of classroom management styles from the very strict to the very loose and everything in between. What I came to realize is I was going to need to find something that could work for me. I felt the strict was too stifling and students were really being compliant and not engaged. And the loose was way too distracting. I am not sure how any learning can take place without some structure. So I began doing research to gather the expert voices. You know, the ones that tell you to be rigid but not too rigid and certainly don't be a push over. You need to stand your ground, but give a little to help them grow. Love them but don't be their friend. Smile but not until after Christmas. And every one of them had a strategy or a program that was going to solve my classroom issues. I tried putting students' names on the board if they acted out. Then added checks if it continued. You get too many checks and you get a detention or sent out. While it worked, it was hard to fairly distribute the checks and detentions. I would unintentionally allow the first few comments to go by and then start adding names once I became annoyed. If you were quick witted you were safe, If you were the students who tried to add a comment after the crescendo of ideas, you were on the board. All of a sudden I was the one deciding what would be allowed and what would not."

Josh nodded and added, "Yeah, almost like rewarding those who got the quip in early and punishing those who came later."

"Right," Alex said enthusiastically. "I was not teaching how to act in a social setting. Instead, I believe the message I was sending was act fast or you are bad. I certainly have been in classrooms of teachers who could effectively teach that bad choices have consequences. But it was not my personality to do it with such authority. I continued looking. I visited one classroom where the teacher used a system to label kids on their level of behavior. It was actually an entire school policy. If a student was good, they wore a green lanyard. If they had made some poor choices but had been working to make amends, they wore a yellow. If they had some recent, serious infractions, they would wear red and if they were really bad, they wore pink."

Josh sat dumbfounded. He did not mean to speak but the shock allowed the thought to roll right out, "Can you say Scarlet Letter?"

Alex nodded, "I know. I was stunned. The teachers loved it though. They said behavior was lower when they had this system."

"Yeah. I bet it worked. Humiliation is a strong motivator for compliance," Josh said.

"A strong motivator indeed. But I asked and never got the answer as to if the referrals were actually down or the feeling of justice was up. To me there is a difference. If you measure the effectiveness of a program or strategy by how we feel because we were able to punish a student, then we are measuring the wrong thing. Instead, we should measure by how many right choices were made. Much harder to do that, but in education we should not be punishing students. Instead, we should be teaching them how to make prosocial choices."

"Nicely said," Josh spoke drawing out the first word and chuckling as though he just watched the second baseman throw a man out from his knees. "That statement makes me think you found your purpose for classroom culture."

"Yes," Alex said. "It was then that I found an audio book, well, actually more of a lecture on tape called 'How to Win at Teaching Without Beating Your Kids' by Barbara Coloroso. In it she talks about our job as educators is to not be a rigid brick wall or a jellyfish. But to be like a spine. Strong and supportive but flexible to bend when the situation calls for it. I started to realize that I needed to teach students how to behave. They come from households that do not have strong role models either because they are working multiple jobs or they do not have the capacity or concern to support the student's behavior growth. Since students spend so much time in school, I figure we have an opportunity to instill some general social norms. I also noticed it did not matter the socioeconomic status or the educational background of the parents. If they were not on the same page with societal norms or did not take the time to correct their wrong choices, the students demonstrated poor skills. That is when I began to realize that the brain is the key to understanding why and how we respond to behavior cues. Just as in reading and math, if we do not find ways to exercise the brain, we cannot expect students to make the right choices." Alex walked to the whiteboard and picked up a marker and wrote two words on the board in capital letters, COMPLIANCE and RESPONSIBILITY. "What I found was that all the strategies I was trying to implement were about me controlling the classroom and asking students to comply with my wishes. By doing this, I was sending the message that I was the ultimate authority and I wanted them to behave this way. They never reflected on or thought about their choices. If they were not thinking, they were not learning. They were simply recalling my wishes. That was not teaching it was telling." Alex went to the board and under compliance he added the bullets AUTHORITY, NO REFLECTION, SIMPLY RECALL. He continued, "I also realized that responsibility is about having the control to make decisions and accept the consequences of those decisions. If I want them to be responsible, I have to give them a system where they decide what needs to happen and then reflect their actions against these expectations and determine how effective their choices were." Alex then wrote under responsibility the bullets, CONTROL, REFLECT, LEARN.

Josh copied the notes from the whiteboard into his notebook. "That makes sense. The person who is doing the thinking is doing the learning. That is the mantra I learned regarding the instruction of content. So why would it not be the same for behavior? I have never thought about it that way."

"I had not either," said Alex. "But now when I go into classrooms, I see that people who have created good learning environments are either deliberate in what they do to establish it or are naturally drawn to make it about the student. Those that are not successful are either so strict or so permissive."

Josh wondered which he was. Before he could get too deep into his thoughts, Alex interrupted him. "From all that I have heard from our colleagues and my soccer players, you run a fantastic classroom. If you are not deliberate, you are a natural."

"Well, I disagree with being a natural," Josh said surprised. "I just have been at it so long, that I have many years of figuring it out until something works. It has taken some time. I wish I would have had someone who could have helped me reflect about it earlier."

Alex continued, "So, with the knowledge that I wanted to start teaching the students how to control their own behavior, I knew I would have to find a system of strategies that would cause them to think about and reflect on their behavior choices so they can learn. That is when I discovered the work of Edwards Deming and Total Quality Management. His work was about processing strategies that would capture input from numerous stakeholders to help design the system for high levels of productivity. The processes originally were created to help management become more effective in the shadow of Japanese manufacturing successes. By using these strategies in the classroom, we can capture the student's thoughts and give them an authentic voice in how the class functions. The processes you have seen me using the last few days stem from Deming's work and modified by educators around the world. The Web is a great resource for new ideas on how to process through system design. This gives students a chance to weigh in before they can buy in."

"And now you no longer have any classroom issues because they are the ones who set the rules," Josh said enthusiastically.

"Oh how I wish that were true," Alex said with a tone suggesting disappointment. "The truth is issues still arise. There is no magic potion in education. Believe me, if there were, someone would retire a gazillionaire. What it does though, is make the student, who makes poor choices, aware that he is actually violating the trust of his peers and not the compliant wishes of the adult. Positive peer pressure is far more powerful than the wish to comply with adults. Teenagers are designed to challenge authority. They need to begin to spread their wings and find out who they are. If this is done in a system designed to give them freedom of choice but controlling for safety, they will respond and accept the consequences in a far more open way. The way students act is not personal. It is biological. But some students have even bigger troubles. They lack the ability to truly reflect and adjust. The system works for ninety-five percent of students."

The bell rang. Josh spun in his seat to confirm with the clock that the bell was what he thought it was. The students were now arriving. "This has been a wonderful start. I am so sorry to take so much of your time."

"No worries," Alex said. "It is helping me get my head around why I have chosen to do what I do with my classroom. It is helping me reflect on what is important to the successful operation of my class.

"Well this is a time for you to prepare for the day."

Alex smiled, "I was ready yesterday. I am going to have the students brainstorm the routines we have and then create flowcharts so they do not need to ask me every time they need to ask."

"Cool," Josh said. "I was planning to be in your room again today and now I have an even better reason." He stepped out of his high chair and moved toward the board. Pointing at the bullets under responsibility Josh said, "I can now watch for how you give CONTROL to the students so they REFLECT on their choices thereby LEARNING what is expected."

With that Josh waved over his shoulder as he exited through the door. Alex began to greet the students with a soft smile upon his face. He was happy that he was given the opportunity to explain himself and that someone as caring and excited about teaching as Josh, had taken the time to ask why he does what he does instead of simply assuming he was right or wrong.

11

SOPs and Flowcharts

The Monday morning bell rang. "Good morning ladies and gentlemen. Glad you are here today. It is really hard to build a community without the voice of the community. I want to thank you all for taking the time from your busy days to help establish why we are in school, our Shared Vision, and also how we will manage our days, our Code of Conduct." Alex glanced toward a student, "Yes Robbie. Do you have a question?"

"Is that teacher going to stay part of our community?" Robbie asked while pointing towards Josh who had settled into what was becoming his usual seat.

"Mr. Bean is an educator on another team. He is here to help me get settled since I am a new teacher. He will be part of the full school community, but will phase himself out of our team and class community. Is that right Mr. Bean?" Alex said using a staccato pattern except stretching the word right.

"Absolutely. I am Mr. Winter's mentor so we work together to make sure he is comfortable at our school and I can answer any questions he has. I will be returning to my own schedule after a week but may come in from time to time to see how you are all doing."

"This is the best beginning to a class I have ever had. Seems he is doing fine," a sarcastic adolescent voice squeaked from the back of the room.

"I agree," said Josh. "I have enjoyed watching you all work. Quite fascinating."

"Thank you, Mr. Bean," Alex said bringing the conversation back to him so he could move on. "I want to begin by looking at our Shared Vision once again." He pointed to the chart hanging on the wall. "I am hoping some of you will volunteer to help make this poster stand out. Take some of your time to add artwork, borders, pictures, whatever, so it looks nice for the class. But, until then, we will have to use the simple lettering. Please stand up." He waited for the class to be rid of the sound of sliding chairs against tile floors. "Please read the Shared Vision to yourself one time and be prepared to say it out loud." He paused a moment and then said, "Lets read it together.

'We are learners, in control of our actions, engaged to grow, and applying knowledge so we care.'

You all did such a nice job on that. I really like the way it sounds. Give your neighbors a high five and then have a seat." Alex spun and turned his projector on. Without returning his glance back to the class he began. "Anyone know how companies keep track of processes they do everyday? You know things like how to open a McDonald's for the day or a Dunkin Donuts? How about how to start a roller coaster at Six Flags?" Alex looked to the class and the students worked hard not to make eye contact with him. Some even stared at the ceiling with a pained look on their face showing just how hard they were thinking. "Okay. Turn to your neighbor and generate some ideas. Think about this as well; If your neighbor was to come over and do chores for you while you went for ice cream, how would you make sure the jobs got done correctly so your mother would be happy. Two minutes." Alex set the timer and the murmur began. He always felt good when he allowed the class discussion time instead of dominating the air himself.

After the timer sounded, Alex brought the group back for a discussion. "So what did you figure out?"

The first student called on reluctantly said, "I would leave my friend a list of what needs to get done."

Remembering to pause to make sure the student had shared all he wanted to, Alex finally said, "Why?"

The student's face shifted looks from the "Oh yeah I got this" to the "Who me? You want more?" He shifted in his seat and then said, "Well, no one is around if I went to get ice cream. So he needs to know what needs to be done. I don't want to take a chance that he does not do what my mom asked me to do."

Alex paused again, "Good. People need to know what has to happen. Does anybody have something different or more on that point?"

The next student called upon shared, "Well my friend needs to not just know what to do but also how my mom likes it done. If they do it differently then my mom will know I did not do it. If that happens, my mom will get mad."

"Awesome. That is very insightful. Not only do we want our friend to know what to do but also how to do it." Alex paused and counted to ten in his head so students had time to think about that statement. He continued, "Companies do not want to have to tell every employee everyday what they need to do. So they create something called Standard Operating Procedures or SOPs. We are going to create some for our class. This way we will have a reference sheet for how to do certain common tasks when we need them." Alex paused again briefly to give the students a moment. "At times in this class you will be working on projects of your choice. During independent work time you may have a question. I might be busy with another student and cannot be interrupted. I do not want you to waste time waiting for me to direct you if your question is something that is routine and you should already know how to do. Think about if the manager of the Red Sox was talking with a new player about his stance in an effort to improve his hitting and Dustin Pedroia came up and said excuse me coach, are we wearing the red uniforms or white tonight. That could make the coach cranky, especially if others keep coming up and asking. The Red Sox have a way to communicate to all players which uniform will be used on which night. It is up to the players to use those procedures to know. Can you imagine if some wore the red uniform shirts while others wore the white. It would look ridiculous." Alex chuckled to allow time for the thought to get into the student's brains. "Right now we will generate a list of routines that happen often in a classroom and that have required asking a question of the teacher in the past. For instance, how do you hand in work? That does not need to be asked each time we have papers to be turned in. You should already know how to do that. Give me a thumbs up if you are clear on the directions." He paused. Looked. Saw at least one thumb at each table. "Good, at your tables, generate the list. Four minutes."

The students got right to work. Alex was happy to see the students getting to work faster as they got more comfortable with each other. It was a good indication that he was setting the right tone for the community. Alex was also well aware that at times the students would not have the initiative to get started when presented with a thinking task. This used to cause panic but now he knew it was part of being human. When he first began focusing on building culture and thinkers, he took the stalled student as a sign that his strategies did not work. But when he began watching professional adults and talking with business leaders, he saw that go-getterness ebbed and flowed and the momentary decrease to achieve was common, unavoidable, and temporary if given the right conditions. He even witnessed it in himself. Now, when Alex saw the apparent sudden loss of control appear, he simply needed to get the students up, stretch, and then give them the directions again. That was usually all it took to get the students' minds back on task. Too often Alex watched as colleagues gave up on good ideas because students stopped doing it. As with adults, student's minds crave novelty and can wander when faced with a routine. We simply need to re-cue the routine and start again. Similar to opening a combination lock. Before you begin, you need to spin it several times to the right to get its gears lined up.

"Alright. What'cha got?" Alex blurted following the four minute session. "Just shout them out and I will write them on the board."

- How to get a pencil.
- How to sharpen a pencil.
- Go to the bathroom.
- Get a drink.
- Do your reflection journal.

Alex interrupted, "Glad some people were paying attention at the end of our very first class and remembered I said we need an SOP for reflection journaling."

The sharing continued. Group brainstorming was like microwaving popcorn. It started with a few followed by a rush of activity before it settled back to a few pops followed by seconds of silence. Alex knew to stop the microwave of ideas once the pops decreased. Wait too long and you are recording burnt kernels of ideas. Alex always added the last idea. "Something students do not usually think of is what to do if I am stuck. That is going to be important as we continue building a learner-centered classroom. You will be working as individuals and groups. You are going to need to have already thought out steps you can take if you do not know something and I am busy with another group. Visualize how distracting it is to have your younger brother or sister asking you questions while you are trying to clear the next level in your video game. Now imagine how difficult it is for me if my attention keeps getting dragged away from helping one group to answer how to get a pencil." Alex paused and looked around the room. He did a slight hop-skip back to the board in an attempt to bring the student focus back. He knew the brain attends to something unexpected. He returned to his directions, "I need your group to choose one of these routines and make an SOP or a Flowchart. While you ponder the one you want, I need to explain the difference between a flowchart and an SOP." Alex approached another section of the whiteboard and then wrote SOP in blue letters. Under it he wrote 'sequential path with one way through'. He took the green dry erase marker and wrote 'Flowchart' and under that wrote a 'path with yes and no decisions'.

"Okay," he said as he turned back to the class, "Lets do a little bit of unpacking of these definitions. An SOP is used when you want to follow a sequence of steps from the first to the last. It is more like procedures. Do this, then this, then this, and so on." As he talked he drew an oval then put a line moving downward to another oval and then a line, then an oval. "That's an SOP. Now a flow chart is different. There are some decisions that need to be made. You ask a question then decide yes or no. If yes you go one way if no you go another. You do this for each step of your routine." He draws an oval with a question mark inside. Then he draws a line coming out each side. He writes yes over one line and no over the other. At the end of each line he draws another oval with a question in it and repeats this process on the other side. "You would have as many ovals as you do steps in this routine." Alex glanced at the class knowing they had seen these before but may have never thought about them or created them. "So a common SOP in the work world would be how to close a cash register at a grocery store. You need to call your manager, punch in a code, open the register, remove the tray, count the money,total the receipts and hope they agree. Or think of Big Papi getting ready for an at bat. He adjusts his gloves, spits once, claps them together, rubs, and then grabs the bat." Alex acted it out, knowing some would be grossed out by the thought of spitting on their hands.

Josh interrupted from the back of the room, "Mr. Winter, what about the way a football team warms up for practice. Some of the boys in here have already started on the team. Do you guys think it is an SOP?"

"Great question, Mr. Bean. Anyone? A team warming-up before a big practice?"

A student raised his hand. "It is an SOP. We follow the same steps every time. Get our equipment on, line up on our spot, do some calisthenics, running and hitting, and then go to our coach for drills. Then it starts to be different or do things that are not always the same."

"That is great. Sounds like an SOP," Alex said while giving the student a virtual high-five. "Once you get into the part of the practice that is specific to a given position, like running back or wide receiver, you are shifting into a flowchart type of routine. You are most likely unaware of the flowchart but I am sure your coaches are asking questions about what needs to be done based on the last practice, game or scrimmage. SOP's happen in a single line while Flowcharts can lead you in different paths." He paused to let that soak in. Silence was a wonderful way to get attention. "Remember these are your first attempts at creating flowcharts and SOPs. Please do not worry about perfection. The most important thing is to get something on paper and then continue editing and tweaking until you like it. Do not worry about making it perfect. Even the first time." While pointing to the hand written note on the wall he read, "Don't let the perfect be the enemy of the good." This was one of Alex's favorite phrases. It helped him through many days. Not every lesson he planned went smoothly. He paused, counted to five in his head and then said, "Unpack at your tables. What does this mean? Two-minutes." With that he started the timer, grabbed a chair, and sat with a group. Alex enjoyed giving students a common saying and then having them build understanding as to what it meant. He also loved to sit in on conversations as students began to construct meaning. This was the sweet spot of learning. This is when you could really get to know who processes quickly and who needs more time. Who are the listeners and who are the outward processors. Too often we tell students what something means. The power of any thought lies in how the beholder builds meaning from it. If he did not get to the table and observe, he would never learn how his students' minds worked.

The timer sounded. Alex jumped up. "So, what does it mean?" Many hands rose into the air. "Yes, Tim, what does your group think our statement means?"

"We thought it was, well, about not worrying all the time about all the stuff that is not perfect. Sometimes you can worry so much that it is not perfect, so you do not share it with anyone or do the next step even though it is good."

"Awesome," Alex said in a falsetto, singing style. "Erin, you had your hand up. Anything else to add?"

"Some of us talked about learning an instrument. From our very first lesson to our first concert in elementary school to our performances now, we continue to improve. But we still performed in all those other stages of learning. We did not wait until we were experts to try it. We even said we did not think you could be an expert without putting yourself out there in the first place. You know. Pay your dues."

"That was a nice exercise," Alex said. "Do not take what others believe something means and think that is the only way. It may mean something different to you. But it also helps to hear what others think. It might inform your thinking or give you another way to look at it. I think, too often, people worry that what they want to do will not be perfect. That somehow it will not work out as planned. So they do not do something. Well, I am here to tell you as an older and wiser human, nothing ever goes as planned. So at some point you need to stop planning and just do something. So, think about your Flowchart or SOP, but then you must pull the trigger and get something done. Each time you look at it or think about it, it will be better than the time before. Humans are really good at continuous improvement. We take what came before, make some small adjustments, and improve it. The person who invented the first cellphone had no idea that the iPhone was possible. And now the iPhone keeps getting better. I believe they are on version five." Alex glanced to the ceiling, wrinkling his brow, as though he just realized something and needed to ponder it hard. "There is a fine line between knowing you are making improvements and not just recreating the same thing over and over again. Movie sequels are famous for losing creativity and instead follow a formula. Take Rocky Six. It was never going to be as good as the original. It was the same old story line rehashed with different characters. Not a plan for improvement." Alex smiled and then asked how many students had heard of Rocky. Surprisingly many knew of the movie but had never seen one. "Okay. Get to work. I will circulate and help. Only your group can determine if it is good so do not ask me. Trust your thoughts and compare against the intended outcome. You might get frustrated but that is where learning happens."

As Alex circled, he discovered what he expected, students were constantly seeking the correct answer. They would use his most hated phrase, "I don't get it." His response was always the same, "It is a pronoun. What's not to get. Think more clearly about what might be concerning you about this project and then phrase it in a question that I can help you with."

If the students could not get themselves off of the entry point, he would offer them a strategy for moving forward. "Start with the end in mind. There is no wrong path to get there, but you want to get there." He knew that if he showed them how, the power of the lesson was gone. It was as much about the product as it was the process. Once Alex realized that the struggle was not a bad thing, the stress of trying to meet all the content standards faded. He could do so much more if students knew they had the power over their learning. Once the students stopped relying on him for the single right path, his ability to cover more learning targets was realized.

The timer sounded and the students groaned, "We did not finish."

"Did you expect to?" Alex responded. "We will pick this up tomorrow. You will be surprised how much clearer your thoughts will be tomorrow. Many times we have breakthroughs if we walk away and return. Place the sheets on the back shelf, grab your reflection journals and answer the prompt on the board, 'What do I know about myself as a learner?' Think about this activity. I let you go through the thinking process. I could have told you what to write, given you the rules and procedures, and specific directions for how to put them on chart paper. But instead I am asking you to create them. Think through them. How did this make you feel?" The timer was set for 4 minutes and the students got to work. When it sounded they grabbed their stuff and high-fived Mr. Winter as they left the room.

Josh was the last to leave the room. He paused, smiled and nodded his head. "That was a great experience. I think I get what you are trying to do. You are not giving them the procedures because that is too easy. Having them think them out causes them to become better thinkers. With something far less challenging then math. If they can do this, they will realize they can problem solve in math. Even if they are momentarily stuck, it is not about their ability to think. They were already successful in doing that. Therefore it must be the new math content and they can make solve it given time. We need to talk more about this but right now I have to return to my classroom." He patted him on the shoulder and took a few steps out of the door. "I will see you at lunch."

"Oh. I have to do some paperwork and forms and stuff. I feel as though I am constantly running."

"Too bad. Well, we can find another time." Josh said as he turned and continued down the hallway. He knew there was more to Alex not going to lunch. And he would not be the only teacher to feel that way. It would still take some time for Alex to step back in and face another wild pitcher.

12

Stepping Back In

It had been four weeks since the first day of school and the last time Alex stepped into the teachers' lunchroom. He was not actively avoiding the opportunity to talk with his colleagues during lunch, but he was not in a hurry to return. He always had a reason for his absence from the teachers' room. There were forms to compile, copies to be made, and papers to be graded. He kept telling them that as the new person it took him longer because he did not quite know the routine. He had convinced himself he was not being rude or trying to hide.

Today, however, was different. The team had told him a week ago that he needed to be there to celebrate and he promised he would. As the team entered the room, the other teachers began to sing Happy Birthday. The lunchroom crew were there in the same positions. George was still wedged into the corner sitting across from his younger looking work spouse. There was the woman who looked like Maid Alice still wearing her lookalike housekeeper's outfit. 'I need to make an effort to learn her name' Alex thought to himself. He then noticed Josh who smiled and gave him a nod that clearly welcomed him back to the teachers' room. Breaking bread as a community has always been an important ritual in human history. Josh held himself responsible for Alex's decision to not be present in the community.

"Wow," was the best expression Kelly could share as she looked at her cake. "You guys are too much." The team sat at their usual table and began to eat. "Nice to have you here with us Alex," Kelly said while smiling.

"I have been busy with all the stuff of teaching," Alex said.

"Yeah," said Smitty, "we all get that. But we miss having you to talk with at lunch. Team meetings are all about business. This is a time to get to know who Alex is as a person. Your fears, wishes, and stories that make you who you are. You certainly have an interesting path and we would all love to hear about it."

"I will try to be better about joining you. I certainly could not miss the opportunity to have cake for Kelly's birthday."

"Hey," came George's voice from his corner, "How is all that stuff going with your students? You know, letting them tell you about how your class should be run."

Josh took a deep breath preparing himself to defend Alex. As he opened his mouth to speak, Dale walked through the door that connected the teachers' room with the cafeteria. "Where is the birthday cake!" Dale said in his usual voice that could easily dominate a room. "Oh, and of course the person celebrating the birthday." He walked over to Kelly, wished her a happy birthday, gave her a fist bump, and grabbed a piece of cake. He noticed Alex sitting with the team, and with his mouth still partially filled with cake said, "Alex, thanks for helping in the cafeteria. Putting that group of students together to create the Code of the Cafeteria was wonderful. Our issues have decreased significantly. Even when we have one, they never amount to more than a redirect. It is as if the students simply do not want to cross the rules and procedures they created. I look forward to working with you on how to keep the code alive."

Looking around at the rest of the faculty, Dale continued, "you should see how this works. What a wonderful way to help manage a group of people. If you have not cycled through the cafeteria lately, go through and look at the signs the students created. We have posters about what it means to be Ready, Respectful and Responsible while in the cafeteria. They are made by students for students, including the actual words written on the posters. It certainly beats having the students sit quietly or assigning them seats. While those have been the strategies of the past, this respects them and deals with the individual rule breakers and doesn't rely on group punishment."

"What do you do with the little buggers who don't behave?" asked George in his well known disgruntled tone.

"Well, George, we have far fewer breaking the rules. When they do we deal with the individual. Most of the time we simply point out how they violated the code and they get back to doing what is expected. If that does not work we can assign them a seat or a lunch detention."

"I, for one, am a big convert to the idea of setting a Code with the kids," said the teacher who looked like Alice.

"Why is that Bette?" asked Dale.

'Yes!' Alex celebrated loudly in his head. 'Bette. I knew that.'

"Two reasons," Bette said with a definitive nod. "First, I have a lunchroom duty and the level of respect I receive after correcting a student by pointing out the code is much higher then years past. Not always perfect, but I do not expect perfection when working with 200 adolescents eating in one room. But they do not argue. It is as if they buy into the code. The second is the students from Alex's team are clearly more able to process and do independent work. As a teacher who sees all the students, I can clearly tell the difference. Their students come in ready to learn, can refocus quicker, and when given classwork, are far less likely to engage in off task behaviors or come unglued if they get stuck. This allows me much more time to work with students who truly need it. I am no longer managing a whole class. I am instead facilitating a group of learners. It is wonderful."

"Hey, Bette, those students are part of my team too," Smitty said with a bit of sarcasm so it was clearly taken as a joke. "But seriously," he continued, "I too have started to listen to Alex and use some of his suggestions in my class. He does not know that, but I have definitely changed my thinking following the first days of school, after seeing how well the students were doing in his class and on our team as a whole. When all the students on our team gather, there is a clear difference from years past. They are more attentive, quicker to come back to focus if they wander, and more polite to each other. I watched as Alex would simply glance their way and they would stop. Almost with an apologetic look in their eyes."

"Still think you all should not turn your back on them," George grumbled. "Once you take your eyes off of them, they will turn to no good. Simply turn to write something on the board and I bet they are throwing things in the classroom. You need to control through authority."

"Man, what's happening in your class, George?" Dale said with a slight chuckle. "Guess I better get in there and help you out."

Josh finally spoke, "I was in Alex's classes as he set them up. They were fun to watch. He was very methodical while also being fluid. I too have tried to do some of the same strategies but I think I am missing the most important factor, the WHY we do it," he said putting an emphasis on the word why. "I am beginning to think it is less about what we do and how we do it. The strategies are less critical then the outcome of our discipline plan. It is about why you do what you do in your classroom."

"What?" Timothy said loudly. He was a new teacher to the middle school. His position as a high school world history teacher was RIFed at the end of last school year. Since he had seniority, he had bumping rights and displaced a new 8th grade social studies teacher. "The why and the how and the what. All this middle level philosophical malarkey. Just teach the damn kids. If they do not want to pay attention, that's their loss. You need to get them ready for the high school. Stop babying them. Stop watering down the curriculum. If you spend too much time on giving them a voice in the classroom, you lose important instructional time. I only have so much time in a day to get them the information they need to be successful."

An absolute silence fell upon the room. While some people may have disagreed with Alex's tactics, no one wanted to return to the days of the junior high. Many had already gone through the middle level reform movement, and those that lived with the changes, knew they were better for the students. This rant by their new colleague actually caused them to reflect upon the changes being attempted by Alex. We resisted the change last time and in the long run, it made us better. So maybe we should not resist this.

Dale broke the silence, "Tim, we are a middle school and we are designed to support the young adolescent."

"It is Timothy and you are not preparing students for the rigor of the high school."

"That is a loaded statement," Dale responded, "and since our philosophical approach to the education of our 6th through 8th grade students is a non-negotiable, I hope you come to see why it is better." Dale looked at his watch. "I best be getting back to the cafe. Thanks for the cake. Happy Birthday again, Kelly." He turned and exited through the door. As it opened the noise naturally generated by a large group of young adolescents was allowed to pierce the more controlled volume of a much smaller group of adults.

Once the door was shut and the volume returned to a low rumble, Josh looked back at Alex and said, "I, for one, feel there is more to your classroom then I was able to observe. We need to talk. How about next Saturday? You and your family come over and let me pick your mind a bit more. We can have a few beers, talk shop, eat, watch the Bruins all while our wives and children entertain themselves?"

"I will check with Meg but do not anticipate a problem. We have met so few people since we moved, I cannot believe we have other plans." Alex took out his phone and texted his wife who had stopped working as an elementary school teacher to take care of their young family. "Oh, and thanks. I appreciated your comments in there."

"I should have done it the last time," Josh said.

"Not a problem," Alex said with a sincere smile. "I hope you are not let down when you learn about how I run my classroom. It is pretty simple."

"The simpler the better," Josh said. "Hope to get the chance to pick your mind soon."

Alex entered his room, paused before turning on the lights and smiled. Even though he worked for the students, he appreciated the positive support shared by his colleagues in the lunchroom. This was not the last time he would feel this.

13

All-Star Break

Five weeks had passed since Josh had gone to see Alex's room. As much as he wanted to be in there, watching him work with students, he needed to attend to the business of his own classes, grades, and assessments. Fall sports were also in full swing so he had coaches that needed answers, games that needed officials, and parents who thought their future All-Star needed more playing time. Time was definitely a limited resource in a school. Josh was excited to have a professional development day so he might have some time to sit with Alex and do a mini check-in. As Josh pulled into the parking lot the sky was as dark as midnight. The hours of the day had already diminished enough to make it noticeable. The school was also dark and quiet. He parked the car, zipped his coat, and grabbed his briefcase. He focused on his breath which was already visible. He loved this weather. Cool and crisp.

Josh went to the teachers' room, started a pot of coffee, poured a cup and then started toward his room. As he entered the hall, Dale stepped in the front door. "Hey Josh," he said in his typical exuberant voice.

"Hey Dale," Josh responded. "Are you ready for the morning? Or is this a district day?"

Dale chuckled briefly, "Well, it's a District day but that makes it more stressful. Since it is held here, I panic more about being the host then I do the developer of the day. I need to make sure the superintendent has the right type of lighting on the stage, microphones, props, and projectors. If they do not work, it stresses me more than preparing a learning opportunity for us."

"Yeah. I get that," Josh said while taking a sip of his coffee.

"Hey, by the way, nice job with your mentor," Dale said. "The support he gave us in the lunchroom is so helpful. Not that we had serious problems, but the place has a much more respectful tone than previous years."

Josh had no idea how to respond. "I did not do anything. He came in that way."

"Don't underestimate your impact on leading people," Dale said in a tone suggesting Josh was being too modest.

"No, really. I did nothing but sit in the back of his classroom and watch him work. I did not offer a single suggestion," Josh said trying to give the credit where it belonged.

"Well, he certainly felt comfortable enough to try some things. You must take credit for that."

Josh humphed and wondered if that was really something a person could take credit for.

"Hey boys," a voice boomed over Josh's shoulder.

Dale noticed him first, "Hey, Kevin. Ready for the crosstown rival this evening? Big game. I am predicting a victory by a touchdown."

Kevin put his hand on Josh's shoulder before he had a chance to turn and gave it a friendly squeeze. "Yeah, Dale, I hope you are right. Been studying tapes and I do fear their kicking game."

Josh shook his head, "What? There is no kicking in a middle school football game. Let alone watching tapes."

"Gees buddy. Just joking," Kevin said.

"Sometimes I worry that you would go to the nth degree if given the chance. Remember, it is a game between 12 year olds," Josh said.

"Maybe. But it is fun to have fun. For some it is important." Kevin smiled at Dale. "Did I hear you guys talking about Alex?"

"Yes," Dale said. "I was complimenting Josh on what a great job he has done mentoring him. Made a difference in our cafe."

"I would agree," Kevin shared. "He made a difference for the football team. Good work Josh."

"I did not do anything. He is what he is," Josh said in another failed attempt to shift the focus from him.

"Yeah, whatever," Kevin said. "I saw him on the soccer field working with his team, building a community. Asking them why they were there and what a perfect practice looked like. He would then use what the athletes created to help control his practices. Everything he did reflected back to the vision of why they were there. I was so impressed with the effectiveness of his practices that I asked him to help me with the football team. I have not had such a level of buy-in to what we are doing. That leads to a much more disciplined team."

"I would second that," said Angela. The group turned to greet her. "My son has talked about how this team is so committed to each other and to a single focus of improvement. He has been playing since he was five and it was always about him. I like that Kevin now has the boys thinking together to reach this vision, as they keep calling it. Nice work, Josh. Alex has a great influence around here."

"Guys," Josh said abruptly, I have not done anything. So please stop giving me credit."

Angela smiled, "We know. But you were so supportive of him before he got here. We are giving you credit for recognizing it. Not for actually teaching him anything. He is new. You could have exerted your will and made him conform. But you did not. You let him show you what he had. Those subtle differences he uses, whatever they are, make his class a community of learners and not a gaggle of students under his control. I met with him as well and took some of the ideas. It has allowed my writer's workshop to be much more independent and effective. Funny, I have been trying for years to find a way to improve my classes. Each time I told Josh to stop worrying about trying to improve, I was also looking to convince myself." Angela was shocked that she finally admitted it. She continued, "Not that I had major disruptions, but the confidence my students now have is noticeable. Not all of them. But definitely better then before."

Josh smiled. "Has anyone ever told Alex about how he has influenced the school?"

"Of course," Kevin trumpeted. I thanked him extensively. Told him that when he is done playing around with that European football, he should join my coaching staff."

Angela included, "Yes. He knows he helped."

"You betcha," Dale said in his best Sarah Palin. "I gotta go. You have done a good job as well Josh. People need to know someone has their back. You are that guy. Don't ever underestimate that."

The group dissolved and headed to their rooms to attempt to get some work done before having to meet in the auditorium for the superintendent's midyear reframing of the District goals. Josh smiled as he passed Alex's room. The door was open and the light was on but Alex was not there. Josh reflected back to the days just before school opened and the anxiety he felt that Alex would not be ready for the students. He remembered how empty the walls were and the arrangement of the desks. Now the walls had a section labeled SOP/Flowchart for everything from how to go to the bathroom, to how to turn in paperwork, and even one on how to determine that a website was in fact a good source of information. The vision the students created on the first day hung in a prominent location. The students had decorated it and made it their own. It was a vibrant place. It looked more like a workroom and less like a perfectly manicured classroom. He did not have fancy, professionally created, and laminated posters. He had student work. It was different.

The room also had new additions. Josh saw something labeled the Action Point Chart (APC) that was well decorated with stickies from the students. There was also a matrix that had what looked like references to the Common Core State Standards across the top, students' names down the left side of the chart, and stickers in the middle. Each student had a different number of stickers and some were even in different places. What could that be? Why did it have student's names on it?

"Hey, Josh," came a friendly greeting from the door.

Josh spun to see Alex entering the room. "Hey, what are these?"

Alex laughed. "You are so comfortable with me you just jump right in to asking me questions. No conversation about the Patriots game coming up this weekend?"

"Sorry," Josh said while smiling through clenched teeth. "But I have not been in your room for a few weeks and I see you have two additional charts on the wall."

Alex placed his briefcase on his hightop table and walked over to shake Josh's hand. "This one is the class's APC. It is a way for students to maintain voice in how the classroom runs. So often we get students to tell us what they think the rules of the classroom are and then never go back to them. This helps to keep the feeling alive that it is their classroom."

"Cool," Josh said as though he was a teenager looking at his friend's new car. "How does it work?"

"It is pretty simple," Alex began but was interrupted by the call to the auditorium for the beginning of the professional development day. "Maybe another time."

Josh quickly grabbed the offer. "Great. I know you and your family are coming over tomorrow. Definitely on the list of things to talk about."

With that, Josh was gone. Alex stood for a moment, shrugged his shoulders releasing a laugh of amazement, removed his coat, and then headed to the auditorium.

14

After the game

"Are you an IPA guy or more of a malt man?" Josh asked as Alex settled into a kitchen chair. Meg and Gloria had gone for a late-autumn hike. Josh's daughter, Sue, decided to go with them. She was about to graduate with a degree in education from the state university. Some thought this was the impetus behind Josh's obsession with looking for improvements to his already stellar approach to teaching. Josh often talked with his daughter about her classes and the new research being shared. This clearly challenged him. The truth though, was that Josh spent his career always looking to improve. He was not just a professional teacher but a lover of learning. He enjoyed being impressed by the successful execution of a tactical plan and then seeking the nuts and bolts of how it was accomplished. Whether it was in the classroom, on the field, or at the grill, Josh loved to extend himself. The tension felt in learning something new and then applying it to a novel situation is what kept him alive. He recognized this same passion in Alex. The two would develop a long lasting friendship.

"IPA all the way. American or English?" Alex asked back.

Josh raised an eyebrow. "Ooh, a fellow beer snob. It is an American version with a citrusy hop profile."

"Good," Alex responded. "I love both. But it feels like a citrus type night. I love to use Cascade whenever I dry hop."

Josh stopped pouring and looked up as though he was just told that the Patriots traded Tom Brady. "Don't tell me you homebrew as well?"

"Yes. I have been doing it for about 7 years. You?"

"15 years under my belt," Josh said. "What is your favorite recipe?"

"Every fall I make a smoked porter for Thanksgiving."

"How about this year?" Josh asked with a sense of excitement.

"Yes," Alex said. "As a matter of fact I will transfer from the secondary to the kegs tomorrow. Then it will be ready for the feast. What is your favorite?"

"I make a double IPA in the spring. Great recipe but takes a lot of patience as it can boil over easily. Once I made such a mess in the kitchen that Gloria has now kicked me to the curb. I can only brew in the garage." Josh paused a moment, did a laugh-cough combination as though he became very embarrassed but also found it quite funny. "Man, it was a sticky mess all over our stove. The sugars burnt and stunk the house something fierce. I can't say I blame her for not allowing me to brew in the house."

Josh continued his pour and walked to the table. "Enough of that for now, although I do want your recipe. We need to get down to business as I want to get inside your head and see what you think classroom management is all about."

"I hope you will not be disappointed. I don't really have a plan. I am not Bob Marzano," Alex said with sincere humility.

"No. Few people are. But you have a way that you approach your work that makes it different. I have been a mentor for 15 years and rare is the teacher who has it under such control with less than 10 years experience. You then take it to a level I have yet to see. It seems to flow out of you. Almost as if it is simply pure."

"Wow," Alex interrupted. "You make me sound like a well orchestrated machine or a bar of soap. I really do not think either is the case."

Josh smiled wide. "That is what today is about. You do have a center you are working from. I know you have read much research on both the brain and education. I know you have been an animal trainer, a coach, and now a father. You are building theories, asking questions, hypothesizing, and then gathering evidence to either prove or disprove your hypothesis. You are doing all of that but are unaware that you are." Josh took a sip of his beer, "Man that is good," he said while gazing at the glass. "What we will do today is begin to formalize the theories you are creating. I would like to share them with other teachers I mentor as they enter our school. Young people need to know how to work a classroom." Josh paused for a moment and then continued, "Actually, some of us more veteran teachers can learn new tricks as well. The sense of community in your room is so easy to see when looking for it. You also worked with Dale on the cafeteria issues. Why did you do that? You must have had some sense that you were onto something."

Alex smiled sheepishly and shrugged. "Actually, Dale and several students approached looking for help so they did not have to be stuck in assigned seats again. I needed to do something since my boss and students asked. There was nothing more to it than that."

Josh took another sip, swallowed and then shook his head vigorously. "No. There really is something. It seems so simple to you that you are not even aware you are doing it. But the beauty is in the simplicity. We need to draw it out. Remember back to the beginning of the school year. You and I sat in your room and you wrote that it is not about COMPLIANCE but about RESPONSIBILITY. You defined compliance as authoritarian with no reflection so it is simple recall of actions. Responsibility was about students having control, so they can choose, reflect on their choice and learn." Alex nodded back at Josh and he continued. "Let's start with what is different today than when you began teaching."

Alex pondered. He knew he could not get away with "I don't know", or "nothing", and he knew Josh would give him the time to think. So he reflected deeply.

"Well," Alex finally said, "the first big shake in my thinking about teaching came when Meg gave me an article about teaching. It focussed on science teachers, but I was able to use some of it to inform my math teaching." Alex's wife, Meg was also a teacher and often shared articles with him.

"What did the article say?" Josh asked.

"The article said that teaching is not about the content or vocabulary of science but about how people think. You know, to use the scientific method to solve problems. It talked about how only two percent of students go on to study science in college.

When I looked at my students the next day, I began to see them as they are. Four of the two hundred students would go to college to study the content I am so passionate about, but one hundred percent of them would need to be educated, world-class citizens. How much content knowledge did they really need in order to make informed decisions in their lives? And on top of that, could they ever possibly learn all the knowledge of all the content areas?"

"How did this impact your teaching?" Josh began his role as the philosopher-teacher forcing Alex to go deeper.

"I began to realize I should not kill the students with definitions and facts. If only two percent study science in college, how many would study math? I was not producing mathematicians. I needed to stop teaching in a way that only produced math lovers. While a small number would study math, all would need math to be successful in what they do. I could not isolate those who were not enthralled with math."

"Good," Josh said. "What did you do differently. How did this cause you to plan differently?"

"I started to think more about thinking and less about knowing," Alex said with a small sense of surprise.

Josh wrote 'INCREASE THINKING / DECREASE KNOWING', on the whiteboard that was placed on the wall behind the table. Alex knew Josh used it to teach his own children math and not something new for this exercise.

Alex continued, "I knew that the person doing the work was the one learning. I needed to begin finding ways to let students think. I realized the job of teacher was not to teach them everything but prepare them for anything." Alex began to tip his glass to his mouth and then was hit with another thought before he could take a sip, "I also know from my animal training days, that if you want someone to learn a new behavior or skill, you must break it down into its component parts. Karen Pryor, one of the world's greatest dolphin trainers called it approximations. If you want to work on your golf swing, for example, break it into pieces and then put them back together. So, work on distance and do not worry about accuracy. Once you are hitting it a good distance, begin working on the accuracy of your shot. While doing this do not worry about the distance. Then, once ready, put them back together and try for long accurate shots. You need to expect to struggle before they take off together." Alex's eyes shot wide open and he began waggling his finger excitedly, "Ooh, ooh, ooh, and she also suggested not training similar behaviors at the same time. Karen discovered that if she was trying to train a husbandry behavior, you know the things animal keepers do to check on the health and maintenance of the animal, she would sometimes get cue crossing and cause the animal to become confused and frustrated. So you might try to cue a specific husbandry behavior, like open your mouth so I can look in and instead get a show routine, like give me a kiss. Not sure why anyone wants to kiss a dolphin but to each his own. This cue crossing turns out to be very frustrating for animal and trainer." Josh sat quietly taking notes as Alex spoke but trying not to interrupt the brain dump that was taking place. "Same is true for humans. The classic example is that someone should not learn a baseball swing at the same time they are learning a golf swing. The two are so similar yet so different. They could become confused in the training of the muscle memory required for success in both swings. Once one is learned, than learning a new one is of less of a concern."

Josh turned to the whiteboard and under 'increase thinking/decrease knowing' he wrote 'Don't teach two new together.' "What do you think. Capture what you just shared?"

Alex looked. "Yes. I use building a classroom culture in the beginning of the year so students get used to thinking on their own and build confidence in themselves that they can in fact solve problems when all is not obvious. Earlier in my career I would hand out the rules and procedures so I could get to the building of math concepts. I would then attempt to teach students how to think for themselves while tackling math problems that were new to them. They would, of course, become overwhelmed and emotions would skyrocket and some would shut down. If I were training animals, they would bite me." Alex paused and chuckled, "Worst thing about it is I would then wonder why these kids can't think for themselves. You know, blame it on the students and not on my teaching. Once I began to separate the behaviors, using something known to most students, like how to behave in a classroom, to teach students how to be independent, they were able to focus less on the content and more on the thinking associated with how to fend for themselves. They would not shut down and blame it on their innate lack of mathematic ability. So, I guess I do it this way because I want them to practice working together to figure things out, before the thinking gets more difficult as we move into new math material"

Josh smiled, "I agree. That stunt you pulled about not telling them which seat number and table they were sitting at but expecting a specific student to get the material from the front of the room, would have caused students stress in my class."

Alex interrupted, "It does. But it is alright because they are not also stressed about learning or not learning math. They have the confidence that they can do it. They have been in classrooms before and know that teachers have ways for students to get the answers. Getting them to process and seek solutions with such simple material also allows them to learn from their peers without judgement. Unfortunately it is not rare to hear 'I am dumb in math', or 'you are so much smarter than me in math'. Both phrases that represent what Carol Dweck calls a fixed mindset. I cannot believe any student would say 'I am dumb at looking for clues.' or 'you are so mush smarter at classroom rules then me'. They may never have done it before, but once it is done they know how to use the surrounding environment to seek for clues. I guess I want them to realize they have the power to find their own solutions. I want them to think that way during math class. The clues are within the problem. Now, combine that with what you already know and try something. Another strategy I used to help students feel safe while reflecting on behavior choices is the reading of children's picture books that have a behavior message. It takes about ten minutes to read and for the students to reflect the actions and outcomes in the story with our class code of conduct. This really gets the students up into their frontal cortexes, you know the seat of reason and control in our brain. And it is done without fear of someone feeling called out.

I am glad we have mirror neurons so we can imagine a situation even if it is not our own narrative."

Josh smiled and wrote on the whiteboard, 'BELIEVE THEY CAN FIND SOLUTION'. Then he glanced up at Alex, what else is it about the way you run your classroom that is something you did not do at first.

"Well, On the first day of school, I would tell the students the rules and then give them the consequence list for what would happen if the rules were violated. I was under the impression that if I did not get control early, they would run all over me by January. Or in George's case, October.

"Good old George," Josh said chuckling. "He has been in the same mood, sharing his thoughts from the same corner of the lunchroom, since he started. He is really a special kind of teacher. Interesting colleague, but a great teacher."

"Yeah," Alex said nodding his head. "The students are smiling as they leave his room. He connects with them in his way."

"He is not as rigid as he likes to pretend," Josh said in a dismissive tone. "He is one of those teachers who has a natural ability to connect with his students. He does not sit in his room as an authoritarian barking orders at his students as he likes to represent himself in the lunchroom."

Alex smiled and said, "I would love to see his classroom some time."

Josh said, "I know he would be open to that. I can talk with him when we get back to school on Monday. Let him know my mentee would like to see his class.

"Great. Thanks." Alex took a sip from his glass to allow the momentary silence to signal it was time to get back to the original conversation. "The problem I was having with my early approach to classroom management was I was not an authoritarian either. When I felt the room had grown to be out of control, I would start writing names on the board. If the students continued to be disruptive, they would receive a check. And I would keep adding checks until it got so bad they were sent to the office. I never really got to the point of sending the students out though. But I would stand at the board, dry erase marker in hand and stare at the student who was misbehaving, daring him to make another comment. Like a gunslinger in the Wild West. The biggest problem though, it was always the same students getting their names on the board. I also had to remember at the end of the lesson to follow-up with my check getters and make sure they did what was expected of them. The consequences were typically one check was a warning. Two checks meant you were to pick up papers from the floor. A third check was a lunch detention, a fourth was an after school detention and then five, you were sent out. I struggled with remembering to ask the violators to do their jobs. I was the one running around all day feeling miserable that I allowed them to 'get away with it'. Clearly there was no follow up. That system did not work for me. And I would argue that it did not work for the student. If it did, the same students would not wind up with their names on the board every day. And it was never bad stuff. They just could not bring themselves back into focus so we could continue the lesson. It was usually after I used some humor to keep the class's attention. I began to wonder what they were really learning? How were they developing responsibility in my discipline system?"

"So what happened," Josh asked.

Alex shrugged his shoulders and shook his head. "I do what I always do. I began to think about it endlessly. In the shower, driving to work, driving home, rocking my baby to sleep, it was always on my mind. I am not aware that I am doing this, but I enjoy thinking about why I choose to do something and why I might consider something else."

"That is the word I want to hit upon," Josh said aggressively. Stopping the conversation by giving Alex a startle. "The WHY you are doing something. You seem like you enjoy getting to the why and less about the how and what."

"Sort of," Alex said, now with his composure regained. "The how and what are important but are meaningless unless you know why you are doing something."

Josh wrote 'Why is critical' on the whiteboard. "Tell me why you think the WHY is so important," he said as he finished writing the last few letters.

Learners Rule

"Well," Alex began, "I read a great book about business leadership by Simon Sinek called 'Start with Why'. He makes a strong argument that in order to change people's behaviors and sell your product, you need to think about why you want the behavior changed. He states there are two ways to change behavior: manipulation and inspiration. Too often in classrooms we are using manipulation. I was clearly using the 'students get their name on the board' tactic as a form of public peer pressure and intimidation. Grades are another way to manipulate. I have actually made the statement to parents that since your child could not attend in class, it affected his grade. He had all the content knowledge but because he could not demonstrate self-control as I deemed it should be, he was marked down. I cannot believe that ever happened." Alex took a moment to regather his thoughts. Trying to be careful not to get on a rant. But that is exactly what Josh wanted. He was waiting for the information to simply flow and that usually came in the form of a rant. Noticing that Josh was patiently waiting for him to continue, Alex figured it was all right for him to forge ahead with his sharing. "The more I reflected, the more I realized I was teaching students through manipulation to get compliance. I was fooling myself that I was preparing them for a future by building their sense of responsibility. This was a tale I told myself to make myself feel better. Control is good for the one with authority. I was so focussed on how to manage behavior that I never thought about why I would write names on the board. I believed it was important for students to learn about behavior because they needed to get their underdeveloped frontal cortexes in shape for their future. Research now tells us that the frontal cortex, the area of the brain responsible for impulse control, planning and organizing, does not fully develop until people are in their early to mid-twenties. I wanted them to be responsible for their choices and reflect on their behavior so it would cause the frontal cortex to work. But I was the one who did all the work. If they violated my rules, they were out of compliance. I was the person who was upset. I wanted them to do the work of thinking and reflecting on why their behavior was a poor choice. If I truly wanted to teach responsibility I would need to say less 'I' and more 'them'. I was going to need to inspire them to make good decisions in class and then have them reflect against the norm. The WHY I discipline students was for them to practice making decisions and reflecting on the consequences. Some people would say that by giving them a detention and then having them complete a reflection sheet suits that purpose. But I would argue that once the student is removed from the environment, they are no longer thinking about the choice they made and instead have turned it over to blaming the 'man' for trying to keep him down."

Josh laughed at the thought of the students raising a rebellion against the 'man'. "Funny how so many of our students think anarchy is an acceptable plan. I am not so sure they get it."

"I don't think we did either. I certainly felt that authority was meant to be challenged when I was younger," Alex shared.

"Yes. And even well before our time. Wasn't it Socrates, way back when, who said, 'Our youth today have bad manners, contempt for authority; they show disrespect for their elders and love chatter in place of exercise'. He even referenced that they tyrannize their teachers. We like to pretend that these problems are new. They are in fact as old as humans themselves."

"Yeah. John Cougar Mellencamp said 'I fight authority and authority always wins'," Alex shared. "Although, Socrates probably carries more weight in the argument." The two laughed. "I would say that most students do not act that way because they dislike adults. They simply feel the need to challenge authority. It is a game with a winner and a loser. I remind myself often that it is not personal, it is biological. Their brains are wired to seek independent control. This causes the need to practice being independent and that often comes into conflict with our need to control. So I don't take it as a personal insult when students act poorly. But I do need to find a way to discipline that truly teaches responsibility and not simply asks for compliance. I want to create an environment that supports the use of their heads to make decisions and deal with the consequences, both positive and negative."

"But what about those who say we need more compliance. That the problem with society is the lack of compliance?" asked Josh in a sincere tone attempting not to sound like a devil's advocate.

"Compliance is a low level skill and requires little cognitive processing," Alex began his defense. "It does not take thirteen years to master it. Most students enter our schools with a sense of adult authority and are expecting teachers to tell them what to do. Also, schools do a fantastic job of building environments to practice compliance even if you remove the authoritarian classroom manager. What I mean is, many structures that are in place to run the school need to be responded to in a compliant manner. For instance, in the lunchroom there is a specific way to get food. This is a no brainer. You must comply with the kitchen manager, line up, and enter from the right. If we get a new kitchen manager, they may change it to have students enter from the left. Regardless of what we did in previous years, you must comply with the new wishes. When the fire alarm sounds, you must get up and exit the building as planned and practiced. It is not the time to sit down, take a vote and then create a flowchart for how to exit the building."

"Great points," Josh said with a smile on his face.

Alex smiled back, "Thanks. I believe if you trust students to comply they will. But you must also respect that they can handle making decisions on how to behave in a class. It all boils down to respecting that they can."

Josh shook his head, "Well your students clearly know you respect them. Truly respect them. They know you want to hear from them and that they have a voice in how the class is run. What is that tool you have in the back of your room? The one with the four quadrants?

"Oh, that is an Action Point Chart or APC," Alex said.

"How does it work?"

"Simple. the chart paper is divided into four sections. One corner is for anything the students want to say that has been positive for them. Typical statements are 'I like the break time in class' or 'I like the capacity matrices so I can work at my readiness-level'."

Josh interrupted, "Their what?"

"Readiness level," Alex repeated as if he was surprised that Josh had never heard that word. "Students working on what they need when they need it and not as a whole class."

"Sounds interesting," Josh said. "We will need to meet again and talk about that. For now, I want to stay focussed on the community feel of your classroom. Back to the Action Point Chart.

"Right," Alex said. "A second quadrant has a spot for students to suggest what they would like changed. You know, deltas. Typical comments in this section are 'due date changes' or 'seating charts adjustments' or even suggestions for upcoming units. The third quadrant is used for questions. Things like 'when is the next assignment due?' or 'Can we have more time for group work' or 'I would like to have the quiet section respected during work time'. Sometimes the questions could be deltas, but we don't haggle. The important thing is that students are using it to communicate with me and with each other through me. The last quadrant is for thoughts. Some might even say Ah-has. Typical are 'I never thought about fractions as division problems' or 'I love the strategies for finding twenty-percent of a number. Find ten and double'. That is how the Action Point Chart works."

"Great," Josh said. "I have one in the back of my room, but it never gets used."

"Well, the trick is to keep it alive. It needs to become part of the culture of the classroom," Alex explained. "I do this by making sure I read the statements every day and if nothing was placed, I let the students know it was empty. If you do not honor it, they will not use it."

Josh groaned, "I tried, but I got some really silly comments. So I stopped reading them. Soon, no comments appeared. Now it sits like a wanted sign in an Old West ghost town."

Alex smiled, "Yes. That happens. But if you stick through the silliness, and let the students know that this wastes their time, those comments stop. Especially after the first time a big suggestion was made and you took that suggestion and adjusted the class. Then the students start to see it as something real and not another thing controlled by the teacher." Josh nodded as Alex finished. "And it is important to know that simply because a suggestion was made you do not have to take it. The students simply like that the idea was aired, you considered it, and rejected it but offered a valid reason for why it does not work for your class. The point is to get them to respect the process and not worry about them liking you because you do what they say."

"Hmmm," Josh pronounced on his exhale, "So what else have you done to help students develop a better sense of responsibility for their behavior?"

"Another wonderful business intended book I read is the Five Dysfunctions of a Team by Patrick Lencioni. In it he makes the statement, 'If you want buy in, get them to weigh in.' Since I want my students to someday have a job, I believe in creating an environment that allows them to practice the skills of being an effective worker. So I think Lencioni's points are valid for a classroom. Not to mention the reams of research on the democratic classroom approach. So, I ask my students to create the Shared Vision for the classroom. As you saw I use an Affinity Process, a tool from Deming's Total Quality Management toolbox. Using a transparent process to capture all voices is important for buy-in."

Josh interrupted, "But that is a lot of kids and comments. Can't you ask and then create them yourself?"

"You can do anything you want. Again the important part here is why you are doing it and not how. You want to do something that says to students I want you to weigh-in. But you have to be truly seeking their input." Alex was hoping Josh understood his important warning. "I have seen colleagues do the process and then create a shared vision themselves using the words they want. They then do the same with Code of Conduct and tell the class these are the new rules. Students rebelled because they recognized the lack of transparency," Alex said raising an eyebrow to help accentuate the duh of the statement. "The students and the teacher both blamed the process and never wanted to do it again."

"Makes sense. Must be the process," Josh stated sarcastically while rolling his eyes.

Alex continued, "Now, can you wordsmith it? Sure. You can and then have the students vote that the words in fact captured their feelings. That passes through my Why lens and lets students feel they have a voice in my classroom. I go the extra mile and have the students create posters using their words, and in their handwriting. Sometimes a little editing is needed to catch spelling and grammar. This way, they cannot question where it came from and if they choose to rebel, they are pushing against the wishes and desires of their peer group. Few adolescents like to do that."

"You do love why," Josh said in a jokingly saucy tone.

"If everything you do can pass the Why test, then you are doing the best you can. The great thing is that I can fine-tune my Why lens as I learn more through research, and my own experiences. If I was set in my ways and accepted a specific strategy as a best practice so I should not stray from a script, I would not be able to adapt. The how and what I do are important, but only after I know my Why."

"I love it," Josh said.

"I only wish I had figured that out sooner in my own life," Alex admitted. "Being centered professionally is very rewarding."

"Tell me about the SOP's and Flowcharts. How do those support what you are trying to do in your classroom?" Josh was interested in discovering the secret behind these tools. It was a wonderful thinking process the students went through to create them, but there must be a greater purpose for their use in the classroom.

"They are wonderful," Alex began delightedly. "Before I used these, I had such a difficult time circulating around the room and supporting students. I was always answering the same questions, 'Where do I get paper?' , 'Where is the homework packet?', 'Can I sharpen my pencil?', and they went on and on. I was always being pulled away from trying to diagnose what was actually happening in a student's thought process, to answer simple, low level, who gives a darn types of questions." Alex came close to shouting the next line, "And even worse was the student who did not even try and would simply sit, wasting time in an off-task behavior, disturbing others and then claim he was waiting for me to come over to his table because he 'did not get it'. That always drove me nuts. The solution in a traditional sense is to increase control. It used to be that the whole class gets the lecture and then they all work on the same packet of worksheets or assignments so I could walk around. It was a controlled environment. But it was also not a good environment for all kids. Some had to wait for the majority of the class to catch up since they got it early while others were forced to move on even if they were not ready. To control the class meant many would just have to suck it up. That was not good enough. I wanted students working at their readiness-level with me having the ability to support those who needed it. So, when I was at a workshop and was introduced to the concept of SOP's and Flowcharts, I knew it was the way to go. Now my classroom has a flow. And the side benefit is that students are given the responsibility to manage their time and learning. They can find the answers to the simple management questions as needed. If they need to go to the bathroom, they do not need to ask my permission, they need to follow the flowchart for a bathroom pass. If they are stuck, they know what to do until I am available to support them. But, these need to happen within a culture of respect for the Code of Conduct. If you do not have a strong culture, you do not have independent students."

"How can you maintain a strong culture in your classroom?" Josh asked.

"It all starts with you. You must show the students that this will be a classroom built on respect for them as individuals with valid opinions. Does not mean you have to do everything they say, but you need to let them share. I have seen teachers earn the respect of their students without allowing them to weigh-in. But those are rare. You have to be the right combination of strict and warm in a consistent fashion for that approach to be successful. However, using specific processes to capture student voice is a way that can work for all teachers. Once students know you care about them and care about what they have to say, the more you can accomplish in your classroom. Then, once the feeling of mutual respect is established, and you have an agreed upon vision for why they are in your classroom, and a code of conduct for how we will act as a group, this trio drives a learner-centered approach. Then you need to work to keep it all alive."

"You mentioned keeping the code alive to your students. I believe you even sang it to the melody of the Queen song 'Keep Yourself Alive'," Josh stated.

"Yes." Alex said. "I love that song and it seems to fit with what I am trying to say."

"How do you keep it alive? I am not even sure I know what that means," Josh shared in a tone of honest ignorance.

"Well," Alex began, "quite simply, you need to keep revisiting it. It cannot become another static document hanging on the wall that gets referred to in the week before break when the students are extra squirrely. It needs to be referred to all the time, even when it is not needed. As humans, we process and absorb so much more when we have a positive sense of how we are doing. If you used a weight loss tracking app, you would stop after the first few weeks, if not days, if you were always gaining weight. No one likes bad news."

"So let me try to clear this up in my head," Josh asked as he lowered his head and raised his two hands as though he was a preacher on Sunday. "You say I should use class time to have the students look at the code, even if we have not had any behavior problems?"

"Yes." Alex said emphatically. "That is key to keeping it alive."

"What do you do?" Josh followed-up.

"I have students self-assess against our code every week. I ask them how they did this week to be Ready, Respectful and Responsible. I have created a half sheet with those words in bold and the descriptors of what it means to be ready, respectful and responsible. Then students..."

Josh interrupted, "I love how you used the school wide code in your classroom code. That gives it a nice tie in."

Alex responded, "Thanks. It is a nice way to have my classroom be different but still tied into the whole school. Now, where was I, Oh yeah, my behavior rubric. I also have two columns, one for the student to rate and provide explanation if they feel necessary, and a spot for the teacher to score. They rate, I rate and we meet to discuss if we are not on the same page as far as how their behavior has been for the week."

"Is it always the same routine?" Josh wanted to know.

"For the most part," Alex said chuckling over the words. "One thing I have learned as an educator is that no student ever deserves the same treatment as another. I love the book on assessing by Rick Wormeli, 'Fair Isn't Always Equal.' This is a great mantra to repeat as you work with students. Many to most of my students do the same routine and some with very little variance in their scores from week to week. Other students need a little more. And, as they say, less is more. If I have a student who is really struggling, I might simplify it for him and have him practice strategies around being respectful only. Then once he has that mastered, have him work on being ready. That way he does not become overwhelmed."

"And frustrated and bite you like the animals you used to train," Josh said now laughing.

"Indeed." Alex responded. "Always a good idea to go home bite free. If you remember the Why you are doing something, in this case hoping students practice and reflect on making pro-social behavior choices, it makes it far easier to adjust the What and the How. In other words, I am not interested if the students can or even do complete the self-assessment. What I care about is are they learning to reflect their choices against the expectations of the group and then adjust what they do when presented with another opportunity."

"Sounds fairly easy to keep it alive." Josh said.

"It is and it isn't," Alex said. "It is easy to do but difficult to remember to do and even harder to make sure keeping it alive stays on the front burner. It is so easy to let slip because we have so much content that needs to be covered. Our focus is usually on how to get kids to know more. What I have found works for me is to do it with the kids. I think teachers need to be reflective practitioners. So, when the students are doing their behavior self-assessment, I can act as a model for students and reflect on how I did at keeping to my Whys for the week."

"What about those who say it is easier to simply give the kids the rules and expect them to behave?" Josh continued pressing, this time seeming more like a devil's advocate.

"I would say, 'How is that working for you?' And also ask them to tell me what their why is. What are they hoping it does for students."

Josh decided to push further, "Well, in the real world they don't get to set the rules. They need to learn to follow them."

"Okay Josh. Now you are simply being difficult," Alex shot back jokingly.

Josh opened his mouth wide, put his hand to his chest and gasped, "Who me? Couldn't be." He chuckled. "Okay. Seriously there are people who believe that."

"Teaching by talking and hoping someone is listening is simply wrong," Alex snapped. "We need to teach behavior. Students are different at home just as adults are different at home. I act much differently with my own friends and family than I do at work with my colleagues and students. We cannot brush it off. We need to increase their ability to practice pro-social decision making in a professional setting. Roger Shank in his book Teaching Minds says it is not about managing a classroom but insuring the cognitive processes needed to manage a classroom are present. That is why the students create the vision for the classroom or our Why for being together, the Code of Conduct, reflect against the code, create the Flowcharts and SOPs, use the Action Point Chart and set their own goals. I have given them the opportunity to use their cognitive abilities to manage the classroom; not left it to the single adult authority to figure it out."

"Wonderful," Josh said enthusiastically as he wrote 'Teach Cognitive processes' on the whiteboard. "Now I think we can find a pattern and discover how it is you go about creating the wonderful culture in your classroom. Let's see. It really centered around the key point that you need to know Why you are asking students to do something. You clearly want them to do the thinking and not be the passive receptor. Everything you do must reflect your why."

Josh drew a center point with the phrase Teach Thinking below it. "That is actually your Why. You are all about teaching thinking; creating learners. Everything you do is about that point." Then he drew what looked like an archery target around the center point. "This target represents all the results that are possible when you consider building a positive culture." Josh labeled the target scoring rings with the phrases he captured during his conversation with Alex. They were, responsibility-practiced/Self-discipline increased, and relationship of respect. "These represent those outcomes you expressed during our brain dump. The bullseye represents the results that get to your why. You can do something that gives you the desired result of classroom control but it does not give you the bullseye of helping students learn to think for themselves. Sort of like the compliant issues. Compliance helps us to control the lunchroom but it does not help in creating deeper neuronal pathways." He then drew what looked like a popsicle about 2 inches in front of the target. He labeled it Culture Focusing Lens. "This is the lens that focuses your HOWS, you know, those strategies you choose to use to create a positive culture. The lens takes the strategy and directs it at the target. Like a ray of sunlight being passed through a magnifying glass to burn a whole in a leaf. Done just right, the leaf burns."

"Thanks for using a leaf and not an ant hill," Alex said in relief.

"I find that type of behavior cruel as well," Josh said and then turned back to the whiteboard. "So what you need to think about is does the strategy you use pass through the Culture Focus Lens and hit the target? Do you get a bull or a hit of lesser value. Sometimes strategies may get through the lens, as it relates to building culture, but it gives no positive results and misses the target entirely." Josh began to settle into the chair. Then, just as his spine hit the back of the chair he sprang forward to continue with his drawing. "Of course, the best is to find a strategy that builds culture so it passes through the lens, and also teaches thinking. That is a bullseye in this case." Josh sat all the way back in his chair and took a few deep breaths. He looked at his creation for a few silent moments and then turned towards Alex, "What'cha think?"

Alex turned his gaze to the board and said, "I do like it. I think it represents what I do when I think about culture. It is

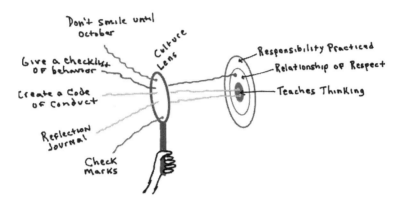

more then managing the Hows. I was taught to manage a classroom, both formally in my college classes and informally in the way I was treated as a student. I think the only piece missing from the diagram is the idea that the teacher acts as the overseer of the culture and not the manager of the classroom."

"Oh I like that," Josh said as he glanced back to the board. "Sort of turns the tables. Not sure how to represent that."

Alex shrugged indicating his uncertainty in how to represent it and then began to talk it out. "Simply managing the pieces of the classroom is too narrow to really build a culture of self-reliant learners. Overseeing is more about surveying or watching for specific outcomes from a higher position and then making necessary adjustments to improve the outcome. In the case of a classroom, the higher position would be more figurative. It would be about observing the culture through the students' reflections and data from surveys to get perspective on how the students are feeling. The overseer position would not come from sitting on a stool hanging on the wall or as the authoritarian boss barking orders from on high. They are the overseer because they are more of the expert in the class. Someone needs to be the final decision maker. Those decisions should be based on student comments, you know, an opportunity for them to weigh-in, but they should be made by the teacher."

"Yes." Josh said. "It is about overseeing the culture of the classroom by surveying the results. If you desire for students to think and respect each other, what better way to do this than check in with them. Obviously done through assessments of the Code and the Vision. Dang, it all makes sense and is totally connected."

"I guess I never realized how connected it all was," Alex said humbly.

Just then the door opened and the families returned from their hike. "Hello," Gloria shouted from the door. "Are you boys working or watching sports?"

"Working, of course. Bruins are not on until 4:25. Late afternoon game," Josh declared. "I think we had a breakthrough. Do you have a minute so we can check our thinking with you and Meg?"

Meg walked in and greeted both. "Let me see what you got." She was always so excited when Alex shared his thoughts and solutions regarding how to work with students. He had good insights. Maybe they came from the way he acted and felt while he was a student in school. He never did fit in with the control environment but had a strong belief in needing to respect others. Alex was a believer that you could be both respectful and independent.

"Take a moment to digest and then tell me what you think is happening. It has to make sense without much discussion," Josh said. He stood up, pointed to his glass and then to Alex's. With a simple nod from Alex, Josh took his glass for a refill. By the time he returned, Meg was ready to give it a shot.

"It seems as though these squiggly lines labeled check marks and journaling, etcetera," she said while pointing to the diagram Josh had drawn on the whiteboard, "pass through this item, which is either a popsicle or some type of lens."

"It is a lens" Josh said in a tone that attempted to defend his drawing expertise.

"Oh, yes." Meg said apologetically. "I can see it. Then, if it passes through the lens just right it hits this target. And it can hit the bulls-eye, hit another scoring ring or miss the target completely."

"Oh, I know," Gloria was ready to jump in, "they are like light waves. You can bend them and make them go in different directions. The hands holding the lens must be the person controlling it. How the waves enter will determine how they are refracted and where they strike the target."

Meg took the conversation back, "The healthier the ray and how it strikes the lens will determine what happens. Knowing Alex as I do, if he were to choose a strategy for management that was strong on controlling with little or no input from the students, it would miss the target completely because you are not creating an environment that fosters thinking, self-discipline, or respect, which are the labels of the scoring lines on the target."

Gloria smiled, "So, I could choose any phrases for the score rings on the target, including the bullseye if I really wanted to. So it is not about having to do a specific strategy, it is about creating specific targeted outcomes that work for you and then making sure you are constantly checking to see if what you are doing is getting the results you were hoping for. Kind of the way I oversee my business."

Josh and Alex looked at each other, smiled large and high-fived. "There is that word," Josh declared.

"What did I say," Gloria asked looking confused.

"Oversee," Alex explained. "We are not looking to manage all the ways the classroom should be run. Instead, we want to oversee how it runs. That requires management but it goes beyond simply controlling the pieces to run as expected. One cannot support working towards a vision if you are constantly managing the old ways of doing things. Overseeing allows you to adjust what you are managing."

"I attended a seminar once," Gloria shared, "and the presenter said the difference between a bureaucracy and a successful organization is that the bureaucracy worries about the inputs and hopes that leads to good outcomes. A well run organization does not care about the inputs as long as you are getting the outputs you desire. How you get there is not as important as if you get there. You must keep it legal and ethical of course.

Alex smiled, "Yes. That is how I have always felt about school. I want my students to blank, please insert your word in the blank. I am not going to follow an exact script but instead figure how to get them there. If I want my students to know how to divide fractions, I need them to learn how to divide fractions. If I want them to think, I need them to learn to think. Anything less, regardless of how wonderful my inputs were, is simply not good enough."

"Well I guess it worked," Josh declared. "Our wives seem to get what we are trying to say. Now you have to show me how to do these strategies. You know, show me your HOWs. How do I capture voice? How do I keep the Code alive, How do you use an Action Point Chart? How do we build a code of conduct in the first place? An SOP? a Flowchart? Still so much to do. Let's get started." Josh began to move items around and organize papers and pens. He looked up and could see the exhaustion on Alex's face and laughed. "Another day. As a matter of fact, I think you should offer a seminar at school in how to use these strategies. Many of our colleagues would appreciate it."

"I would love to," Alex said. "But, lets make sure we start with WHY we want the training. That will be our bullseye."

Lenses of Customized Learning

CULTURE

- Growth mindset is evident with teachers and students.
- Reflective Learners
- Celebrations of Learning
- Voice - Students have an active role in creating and maintaining the culture of the classroom/team: moving from compliance to responsibility.
- Motivation = Autonomy + Mastery + Purpose. (Pink, D. 2011. Drive)
- Welcoming and safe environment
- Errors in thinking are welcome and students are explicitly taught how to discard incorrect information and understandings
- Respects differences. Students are in different places in their learning and that is OK.
- Relationship focused. Community building.

FACILITATION / INSTRUCTION

- Applied Learning. Knowledge is applied and not simply assessed. Students are active doers and not passive knowers.
- Student choice based on interests
- Instruction is aimed at a student's Zone of Proximal Development. Grouped for readiness.
- Explicit Instruction of content, skills, habits of mind and reasoning processes.
- Workshop model
- Understanding of Input---> Reasoning ---> Output
- Physical area supports student-centered learning (resource area, meeting area, etc)
- Integrated units
- Coaching

CURRICULUM
- Well defined continuum of learning
- Transparent
- Includes H.O.W.L.s (Habits of Work and Learning)
- Includes complex reasoning skills

ASSESSMENT
Good assessment provides evidence of learning which
- is tied to targets at the correct reasoning level
- informs our instruction
- may not look the same for every student
- makes progress visible to students
- directs effective feedback

MAMS January, 2013

Sharper focus on the Culture Lens

Places in the narrative where Alex and the others demonstrated or discussed establishing and maintaining a strong culture of learners.

Growth Mindset is evident with teacher and students.

- OK to be innovative as discussed by Gloria and how she grew her coffee shop.
  - Steps to do it:
    - set a vision.
    - identify where you currently are on the continuum ranging from nothing to your actual vision.
    - design your steps to bridge the gap.
    - operationalize your ad-hoc measures.
    - execute steps and watch for trends that you are getting closer to your vision.
- Alex is always seeking chances for his students to turn and talk. When students seem confused or have a disagreement, he knows those are great times for students to think, pair, share or do another processing activity.
- It is about the process and not the product. Effort is what pays off.
- Alex uses the classroom rules and procedures to teach the basics of collaborative problem solving because students are familiar with how a classroom runs. That way, when the students get to problem solving in math, they are already confident that they can.

- BELIEVE THEY CAN FIND A SOLUTION is one of the key points recorded by Josh during Alex's brain dump.

Errors in thinking are welcome and students are explicitly taught how to discard incorrect information and understandings

- Alex always looks to supplant places where teachers do the telling with places where students do the thinking.
- Alex begins the year with an easy problem solving strategy. He creates his Seating Chart by using a calendar he has cut into pieces. Students make inferences that the whole picture in the middle of the table must mean that is their group. Trial and error.
- Alex tells the Students in seat #2 to get the bin for their table. Alex then lets the students know it would be their job to find clues in their surroundings to answer the problem. Trial and error.

Relationship focused. Community building

- On day one, Alex had the students introduce themselves and asked them to share their strengths. This breaks down barriers between people. Alex kept track of their strengths throughout the year to help the learner when they struggled with new learning.
- Alex discusses his knowledge of learning and says that to build on a strength, use material more familiar so they are not struggling with multiple parts.
- Alex explicitly asks his students to help those who are confused. He knows he needs to make them aware of their responsibility to others in their community. At the same time he walks around so the students are not the only path to understanding.
- Alex creates Strength Charts throughout the year when they get to new material.
- Alex teaches the students how to ask for a person's name and lets them know it is all right to not remembering them all.

- Alex talks about the lanyard system. His message is clear: Don't punish students. He wants them to make pro-social choices.
- Not group punishment but group expectations. Deal with the rule breakers as individuals. Respect the group. Remember that most kids do the right thing. Also most adults would not put pressure on someone to stop doing the wrong thing. Don't expect adolescents to be able to pressure peers.

Students are in different places in their learning and that is OK. Respects differences.

- Alex circulated the room and helped the students who were unclear instead of repeating the directions and frustrating those who already understood.
- Alex used a Wall Chart to track student progress through learning outcomes. The community accepts as a means of showing progress and that their location on the chart is representative of where they are in their learning. Some may be ahead and some may be behind and that is OK.
- Alex tries to not use manipulation through grades and public discipline to encourage the right behavior choices. Instead he focuses on inspiration as discussed by Simon Sinek in his book Start With Why. (See references)
- Alex demonstrates his belief that fair isn't aways equal when he adjusts the weekly behavior reflection requirements. Sometimes kids need more by being given less on which to focus.

Voice - Students have an active role in creating and maintaining the culture of the classroom/team: moving from compliance to responsibility

- Alex is always on the lookout for strategies he can use to capture voice such as: how much more time do you need, fist to five, colored cups, Thumbs-up/ Thumbs-down, Secret Acceptance Chart, Action Point Charts.

- Alex creates a Code of Conduct with his students versus already having the rules on the wall.
- Alex creates a Shared Vision for the class. Why is so important to him, that he wants the students to know Why they are in his class or on his soccer team?
- Alex trusts his students can make good behavior decisions.

Reflective Learners

- Alex has his students keep a reflection journal.
- He develops ways for his students to think about their behavior and compare their choices against the class expectations.
- He wants his discipline plan to be about teaching responsibility and not about demanding compliance.
- Compliance = control, no reflection so it is simple recall of actions; Responsibility = choice, reflection, learn.
- Alex reads a picture book to his students and has them compare it to their Code of Conduct.
- WHY IS CRITICAL (written by Josh as one of Alex's ideas during the brain dump.) "The how you do it" and "what are the results" follow your why.

Welcoming and safe environment

- Alex greets them at the door with a smile on his face from day one. He remembers his first principal saying, "Culture begins at the door on day one. Don't miss it." He never has.
- Alex uses humor without cutting down on a student. He only teases himself but models self-respect.
- Alex ends each class with a sign of appreciation for their time together
  - Thanks for the day
  - I enjoyed the learning that took place in here today
  - Have a great Wednesday
- He uses dice to mimic a random number generator. The dice called on the students and not the teacher.

Neuroscience pieces

- Teacher's job is to create the conditions for the students to learn. That is what is constantly on Alex's mind and he shares with Josh in the chapter, New Way to Pitch. He needs to create an environment for students to practice cognitive skills.

- Have students unpack and build understanding of common sayings and quotes. The power of any thought lies in how the beholder builds meaning from it.

- Learning happens in the frustration - Alex tells his students when they are working on SOPs and Flowcharts. He encourages them to trust their thoughts and compare them against the intended outcomes. This is a good strategy for getting things done.

- When his students say "I don't get it," he says 'it' is a pronoun and then encourages them to better define what they don't get.

- Alex believes the job of an educator is to not teach our students everything but prepare them for anything.

- Josh records Alex's bullseye for why he does what he does; INCREASE THINKING / DECREASING KNOWING.

- Alex and Josh discuss the rebellious side of adolescents and Socrates' comments. This leads Alex to comment that student behavior choice is biological and not personal. Adolescent brain wiring is designed for them to question authority.

- The TRIO of Learner-centered Classrooms are (1) Shared Vision (Why), (2) Code of Conduct, and (3) mutual respect built through the use of voice capturing processes.

The Tools

Creating a Shared Vision:

> Our vision for Casco Bay is for our students to excel in our learning, team skills, and friendship. We shall stay side by side improving our weakness and fixing our problems. What is the most important is getting ready for the high school down the road, but we will not forget the importance of teamwork and relationships. Casco Bay is a productive family that won't give up to any tough even when things may be hard, and we will push ourselves to our limits. Casco Bay was molded to do anything nothing is or is impossible. Every Subject and obstacle can be overcome. Day by day we will grow, we will achieve, and we will Succeed.

Purpose:
- To establish WHY the community is gathered. What is the reason to come together. Gives the classroom a common identity that can be referred to and reflected against. Are we meeting our shared vision?
- Allows all students a chance to weigh in before asking them to buy in to the purpose of the class.

Important to remember:
- Should be created by the students. Teachers can help wordsmith to improve the spelling, grammar or flow, but it should be in student language and not teacher voice.
- Have the students create the poster

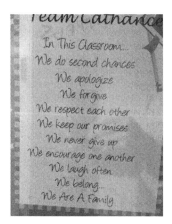

In This Classroom...
We do second chances
We apologize
We forgive
We respect each other
We keep our promises
We never give up
We encourage one another
We laugh often
We belong...
We Are A Family

with the Vision on it. Should represent their work and not a professionally done poster.

- Should be done each year. If you loop (keep the same students for more then a single year) you should revisit the vision and determine that it is still the goal of your class.

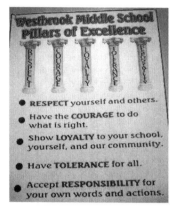

- As you are going through the process, watch for students who are not an active part. All must feel they had a chance to be heard. If a student is silent, go to the group and the student directly for his or her thoughts. Asking for input from a reluctant member is also good modeling for those students who are comfortable sharing.

Steps:
Affinity Process

1. Write the prompt you want students to respond to: (examples)

What does a good classroom look and sound like?

or

What does a successful learner look and sound like?

2. Students should brainstorm ideas and write them on stickies. They should use a new sticky for each idea. This should be done as individuals without talking.

3. Students group similar comments in like categories. This should be done without talking.

4. Finally, have the students label the categories with a word or phrase that summarizes all the words below.

This can be done while talking. Students may want to move their Stickies to better fit a category.

5. Once all groups and classes have had a chance to do the Affinity Process, have a representative group wordsmith using all of the categories to get down to a single phrase that should be voted on for acceptance as the Shared Vision.

WUC - Write, Underline, Create

1. Individually - write 1 or more statements explaining **what a good classroom would look or sound like** (replace bold text with your driving question). 5-10 minutes quiet time. (adjust time for your group's capacity and need)
2. Pass your paper to the person on your left.
3. Underline any statements or words which are significant to you.

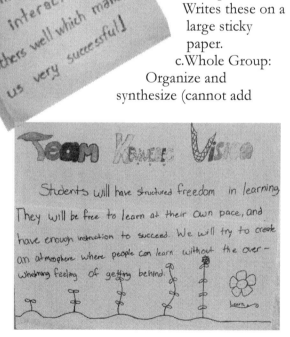

4. Continue passing until you have read and underlined on each person's paper in your group.
5. Create 1 group synthesis of ideas:
   a. Group Reader: Reads statements with 2 or more underlines.
   b. Group Recorder: Writes these on a large sticky paper.
   c. Whole Group: Organize and synthesize (cannot add

anything new nor can ignore any
statements.

d. Group reporter: Read final statement to
entire group.

e. Whole group Shared Vision can be
created using the same process or
wordsmithed by a representative group
and then voted on.

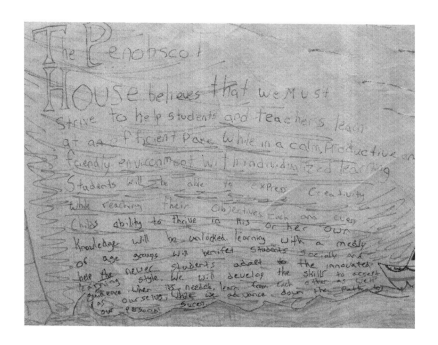

Acceptance Chart Vote (Secret or Public)

Purpose:

- To gain an understanding of the student's commitment to an idea or concept. It can be a simple linear vote, say from 0 to 100 or it can be more of a matrix with one variable on the x-axis and another on the y-axis.
- It is also a great way to capture the understanding or feeling of the group as they begin a new unit or move into working with new information.

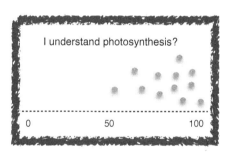

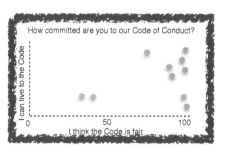

Important to Remember:

- It can be done as a secret or a public vote. If anonymity is required, remember to put a few colored dots on the chart and then do not allow others to use that color. This maintains the integrity of the early voters. If not possible to add a few early votes, Ask for volunteers to go first. I have never had someone refuse to step up.
- Share the results and be ready to have the results inform the next steps. People do not like voting for the sake of voting. It must be used to give insight into some action.

Steps:

1. Create the chart. Decide if it is a single response or a double axis response.
2. Label the axis so the participants are clear on what they are voting on.
3. Give students something to vote with (Dots, Stickies, Markers, etc.)
4. Let students move to the chart (movement is good for the mind)

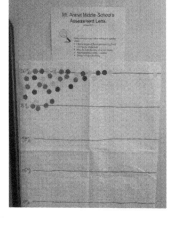

5. Share the results and discuss how it informs the next steps in their learning or classroom design.

Creating a Code of Conduct

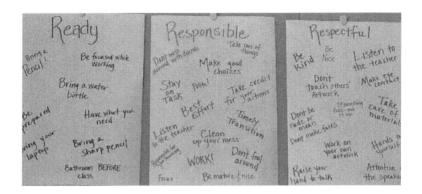

Purpose:

- To help students feel they have an opportunity to weigh-in before they are asked to buy-in to the structure of the class.
- Sets positive expectations that students can reflect against to build a stronger sense that they are in control of their actions.

Important to Remember:

- Should be in positive statements or expectations. These are what we want students to do and should not be a list of "thou shall nots".

- Statements need to be in student friendly language. If they do not know what it means they cannot be expected to do it.
- The code is only as

effective as you keep it alive. The code is not meant to be a static document that sits on the wall and referred to only once the class is out of hand. It is something students need to reflect against, daily or weekly, depending on your style and the students' needs.

Steps:

1. If your school has already gone through the process of creating a 3-5 word matrix for school-wide positive behavior expectations, use those words. If you do not have one, work with your administration to put one in place. See the references for information on Positive Behavioral Interventions and Supports (PBIS.org). You can also use the key words

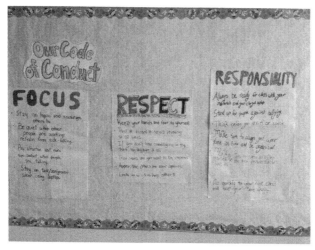

described in the classroom shared vision you created.

2. Have students brainstorm actions that would show visitors we are living up to our code. Keep it to 3-5 statements or actions. Have them choose a single word or phrase, like Focus or Respect and then add the descriptions of behaviors that would signal

meeting the Code. They should not try to find actions that meet all the words in your Behavioral Matrix.

3. Have students make charts or posters using their own words that will be hung in the classroom as a constant reference.

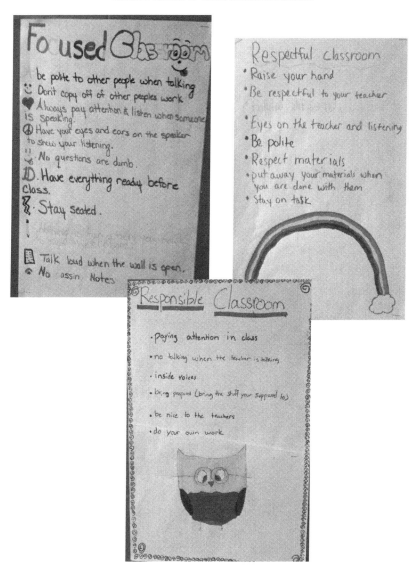

Voice and Choice Classroom Processes

Action Point Chart (APC):

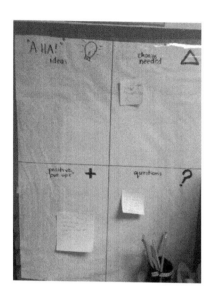

Purpose:

- To give students continuous opportunities to weigh-in so they can buy-in.
- Students can anonymously express what is working and what needs to change as well as ask questions or share insights with the teacher and the whole class. Students will let you know the points they would like to see some actions to resolve.
- Makes your classroom more about the responsibility of the learner and less about the compliance of the student.

Important to Remember:

- You must acknowledge the notes on the Action Point Chart in a consistent and timely way manner. If students thoughts are allowed to sit, they will stop using the tool.
- You must acknowledge the ideas. This does not mean you have to make the changes, but you need to let students know why the suggestion will not work in your classroom.
- Silliness will fade if you are being true to the tool. If students see that they have input into how the class runs, they will want to share their thoughts.

Steps:

Simply divide a piece of chart paper or a section of your board, into four quadrants. Label one quadrant Questions, another Changes, another Positives and the last with A-Ha's.

Standard Operating Procedures (SOP's)

Purpose:

- To give students a visual reference for what steps are involved with routine classroom procedures.

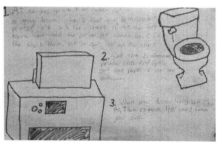

- Frees the teacher from having to answer or explain the same routines so he/she is able to focus on those students needing help building relevance about the content.
- SOP's are used for procedures that follow a set sequence of steps.

Important to Remember:

- Whenever possible and appropriate, have the students create the charts in their own words. This takes away the "I did not know what it meant" reason for not following the procedure.
- Use positive or emotionally neutral statements. Avoid the "Thou Shall not" approach to management.

Steps:

Have students visualize the outcome. Then have them create the steps from beginning to end. I have the students run through the steps to check for accuracy and ambiguity before they put them on chart paper or poster board. Students like to get right to it and create the end product without first making a draft.

Flowcharts

Purpose:

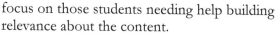

- To give students a visual reference of what steps are involved with routine classroom procedures.
- Frees the teacher from having to answer or explain the same routines so he/she is able to focus on those students needing help building relevance about the content.
- Flowcharts are used for procedures that could have more than a single path depending on the answer to a series of yes/no questions.

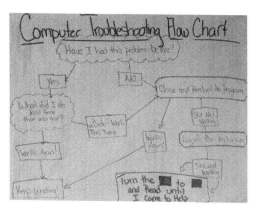

Important to Remember

- Whenever possible and appropriate, have the students create the charts in their own words. This takes away the "I did not know what it meant" reason for not following the procedure.
- Use positive or emotionally neutral statements. Avoid the "Thou Shall Not" approach to management.

Steps:

Have students visualize the outcome. Then have them create the steps from beginning to end. I have the students run through the steps to check for accuracy and ambiguity before they put them on chart paper or poster board. Students like to get right to it and create the end product without first making a draft.

REFERENCES

Alexander, W. M., Carr, D., & McAvoy, K. (2006). *Student-oriented curriculum: a remarkable journey of discovery*. Westerville, OH: National Middle School Association.

Ariely, D. (2008). *Predictably irrational: the hidden forces that shape our decisions*. New York, N.Y.: HarperCollins Publishers.

Ariely, D. (2012). *The (honest) truth about dishonesty: how we lie to everyone--especially others*. New York: Harper.

Ark, T. V. (2011). *Getting smart: how digital learning is changing the world*. San Francisco: Jossey-Bass.

Bransford, J. (2000). *How people learn: brain, mind, experience, and school* (Expanded ed.). Washington, DC.: National Academy Press.

Brookhart, S. M. (2010). *How to assess higher-order thinking skills in your classroom*. Alexandria, Va.: ASCD.

Caine, R. N., & Caine, G. (1994). *Making connections: teaching and the human brain*. Menlo Park, Calif.: Addison-Wesley Pub. Co..

Cozolino, L. J. (2013). *The social neuroscience of education: optimizing attachment and learning in the classroom.* New York: W.W. Norton & Co..

Curwin, R. L., Mendler, A. N., & Mendler, B. D. (2008). *Discipline with dignity new challenges, new solutions* (3rd ed.). Alexandria, VA: Association for Supervision and Curriculum Development.

DeLorenzo, R. A. (2009). *Delivering on the promise: the education revolution.* Bloomington, IN: Solution Tree.

Dehaene, S. (1997). *The number sense how the mind creates mathematics.* New York: Oxford University Press.

Doyle, T. (2011). *Learner-centered teaching: putting the research on learning into practice.* Sterling, Va.: Stylus Pub..

Drake, S. M., & Burns, R. C. (2004). *Meeting standards through integrated curriculum.* Alexandria, Va.: Association for Supervision and Curriculum Development.

Duhigg, C. (2012). *The power of habit: why we do what we do in life and business.* New York: Random House.

Dweck, C. S. (2006). *Mindset: the new psychology of success*. New York: Ballantine Books.

Fisher, D., & Frey, N. (2012). *How to create a culture of achievement in your school and classroom*. Alexandria, Va.: ASCD.

Gallup Student Poll. (n.d.). *Gallup Student Poll*. Retrieved July 5, 2013, from http://www.gallupstudentpoll.com/home.aspx

Gladwell, M., & Gladwell, M. (2000). *The tipping point: how little things can make a big difference*. Boston: Little, Brown.

Gladwell, M. (2008). *Outliers: the story of success*. New York: Little, Brown and Co..

Goldberg, E. (2009). *The new executive brain: frontal lobes in a complex world*. Oxford: Oxford University Press.

Goleman, D., Boyatzis, R. E., & McKee, A. (2002). *Primal leadership: realizing the power of emotional intelligence*. Boston, Mass.: Harvard Business School Press.

Goleman, D. (2007). *Social intelligence: the new science of human relationships* (Bantam trade pbk ed.). New York, N.Y.: Bantam Books.

Greene, R. (2012). *Mastery.* New York: Viking.

Hamel, G. (2012). *What matters now: how to win in a world of relentless change, ferocious competition, and unstoppable innovation.* San Francisco, CA: Jossey-Bass.

Hargreaves, A., & Fullan, M. (2012). *Professional capital: transforming teaching in every school.* New York: Teachers College Press.

Heath, C., & Heath, D. (2010). *Switch: how to change things when change is hard.* New York: Broadway Books.

Heath, C., & Heath, D. (2013). *Decisive: how to make better choices in life and work.* New York: Crown Business.

Home. (n.d.). *Positive Behavior Interventions and Supports.* Retrieved June 25, 2010, from http://www.pbis.org/

Public Television. (n.d.). Brandon Busteed of Gallup. *Iowa Public Television.* Retrieved February 5, 2014, from http://

www.iptv.org/video/detail.cfm/31988/

itt_20130113_brandon_busteed

Jensen, E. (2008). *Enriching the brain: how to maximize every learner's potential.* San Francisco, Calif.: Jossey-Bass ;.

Jensen, E. (2009). *Teaching with poverty in mind what being poor does to kids' brains and what schools can do about it.* Alexandria, Va.: Association for Supervision and Curriculum Development.

Jones, F. H. (1987). *Positive classroom discipline.* New York: McGraw-Hill.

Kahneman, D. (2011). *Thinking, fast and slow.* New York: Farrar, Straus and Giroux.

Khan, S. (2012). *The one world schoolhouse: education reimagined.* London: Hodder & Stoughton.

Kohn, A. (1999). *The schools our children deserve: moving beyond traditional classrooms and "tougher standards".* Boston: Houghton Mifflin Co..

Lehrer, J. (2009). *How we decide*. Boston: Houghton Mifflin Harcourt.

Lencioni, P. (2012). *The advantage: why organizational health trumps everything else in business*. San Francisco: Jossey-Bass.

Levy, S. (2011). *In the plex: how Google thinks, works, and shapes our lives*. New York: Simon & Schuster.

Marzano, R. J., Pickering, D., & Pollock, J. E. (2001). *Classroom instruction that works: research-based strategies for increasing student achievement*. Alexandria, Va.: Association for Supervision and Curriculum Development.

Marzano, R. J., Marzano, J. S., & Pickering, D. (2003). *Classroom management that works: research-based strategies for every teacher*. Alexandria, VA: Association for Supervision and Curriculum Development.

Marzano, R. J. (2007). *The art and science of teaching a comprehensive framework for effective instruction*. Alexandria, Va.: Association for Supervision and Curriculum Development.

Marzano, R. J., Pickering, D., & Heflebower, T. (2011). *The highly engaged classroom*. Bloomington, IN: Marzano Research.

McTighe, J., & Wiggins, G. P. (2013). *Essential questions opening doors to student understanding*. Alexandria, Va.: ASCD [Association for Supervision and Curriculum Development].

Nunley, K. F. (2001). *Layered curriculum: the practical solution for teachers with more than one student in their classroom*. Kearney, NE: Kathie F. Nunley.

Patterson, K. (2002). *Crucial conversations: tools for talking when stakes are high*. New York: McGraw-Hill.

Pink, D. H. (2011). *Drive: the surprising truth about what motivates us*. New York: Riverhead Books.

Pink, D. H. (2012). *To sell is human: the surprising truth about moving others*. New York: Riverhead Books.

Pollock, J. E. (2007). *Improving student learning one teacher at a time*. Alexandria, Va.: Association for Supervision and Curriculum Development.

Ravitch, D. (2011). *The death and life of the great American school system: how testing and choice are undermining education* (Revised and expanded ed.). New York: Basic Books.

Robinson, K., & Aronica, L. (2009). *The element: how finding your passion changes everything.* New York: Viking.

Rock, D. (2009). *Your brain at work: strategies for overcoming distraction, regaining focus, and working smarter all day long.* New York: Harper Business.

Schank, R. C. (2011). *Teaching minds: how cognitive science can save our schools.* New York: Teachers College Press.

Schmoker, M. J. (2006). *Results now how we can achieve unprecedented improvements in teaching and learning.* Alexandria, Va.: Association for Supervision and Curriculum Development.

Schmoker, M. J. (2011). *Focus elevating the essentials to radically improve student learning.* Alexandria, Va.: ASCD.

Schwahn, C. J., & McGarvey, B. (2012). *Inevitable: mass customized learning - learning in the age of empowerment.* San Bernadino, CA: Chuck Schwahn & Bea McGarvey.

Sinek, S. (2009). *Start with why: how great leaders inspire everyone to take action.* New York: Portfolio.

Sousa, D. A. (2009). *How the brain influences behavior: management strategies for every classroom.* Thousand Oaks: Corwin Press.

Sousa, D. A. (2010). *Mind, brain, and education: neuroscience implications for the classroom.* Bloomington, IN: Solution Tree Press.

Sousa, D. A., & Tomlinson, C. A. (2011). *Differentiation and the brain: how neuroscience supports the learner-friendly classroom.* Bloomington, IN: Solution Tree Press.

Sousa, D. A. (2012). *How the brain learns* (4th ed.). Thousand Oaks, Calif.: Corwin Press.

Spencer, J. (2008). *Everyone's invited!: interactive strategies that engage young adolescents.* Westerville, Ohio: National Middle School Association.

Tomlinson, C. A., & Imbeau, M. B. (2010). *Leading and managing a differentiated classroom.* Alexandria, Va.: ASCD.

Tool time: choosing and implementing quality improvement tools. (2003). Molt, U.S.: Langford International.

Tough, P. (2013). *How children succeed: grit, curiosity, and the hidden power of character* (Reprinted. ed.). New York: Mariner Books.

Wagner, T., & Compton, R. A. (2012). *Creating innovators: the making of young people who will change the world.* New York: Scribner.

Weinberger, D. (2011). *Too big to know: rethinking knowledge now that the facts aren't the facts, experts are everywhere, and the smartest person in the room is the room.* New York: Basic Books.

Wolk, R. A. (2011). *Wasting minds why our education system is failing and what we can do about it.* Alexandria, Virginia, USA: ASCD.

Wong, H. K., & Wong, R. T. (1998). *The first days of school: how to be an effective teacher* ([2nd ed.). Mountainview, CA: Harry K. Wong Publications.

Zmuda, A. (2010). *Breaking free from myths about teaching and learning innovation as an engine for student success.* Alexandria, Va.: ASCD.

About the Author:

Bill Zima began his career as a zoo educator creating and delivering learning opportunities for students in their schools and guests at the Phoenix Zoo and Disney's Animal Kingdom. Seeking something that was a bit more dynamic, he became a 7th grade science teacher. He is currently a middle school principal. Bill is also an original member of the Maine Cohort for Customized Learning, an organization dedicated to the promotion of learner-centered, proficiency-based education systems in Maine as well as a board member for the Maine Association for Middle Level Education. He lives with his wife and two children in Portland, Maine.

For ideas to help lead Book Talks with Learners Rule, please refer to the information on the website.

Learnersrule.com